THE FOUR PILLARS
OF A FULL SPECTRUM LIFE

A Guide To Living Life At A Higher Level

Claire Cameron

www.FullSpectrumLife.org

BRIDGE PUBLISHING UK

Est. 2010

First published in Great Britain 2014 by:

BRIDGE PUBLISHING COMPANY (UK) LTD

Westfield Lakes, Far Ings Road,
Barton upon Humber, North Lincolnshire
DN18 5RG
England

THE FOUR PILLARS OF A FULL SPECTRUM LIFE

ISBN 978-0-9567066-7-6

A copy of this book has been registered with the British Library.

Book typeset by:
BRIDGE PUBLISHING COMPANY (UK) LTD
www.bridgepublishinguk.co.uk

Printed in England

CONTENTS

Preface

I am chuckling to myself as I write these first words of what I hope will be an informative and inspirational book. I'm chuckling as I think of the English teachers I had at Selby Grammar School back in the 1970's in small town northern England. All but one would be totally amazed to see me sitting down to write a book! Mathematics and Science were my subjects, not English, or anything else descriptive for that matter. Only one of my English teachers appreciated my style, Mr. Eric Taylor, a published author himself. So here's to you Mr. Taylor!

What is the inspiration behind this book? Two things have made me sit down and start to write. Firstly, I have always wanted to make a difference with my life. Always felt that there was something I am supposed to do with this precious life and the gifts and skills I have been given. As I get older, more experienced and more aware, I have begun to realize that I can make a difference to all kinds of people by sharing my experience… sharing the knowledge, clarity and awareness I have accumulated so far and by taking the risk of putting my story and my understanding "out there".

I have been privileged to have known and been influenced by some wise teachers in my life. This book contains an accumulation, compilation and interpretation of what I have learned by combining their teaching and my own experiences. Some of those teachers I have spent time with in person, others I "know" through their books and audio programmes. Some are names that many of you will recognize. Others are simply wise people going about living their lives in a way that has touched and taught me.

The second reason relates to my late husband, Doug Cameron. He will feature strongly in this book. He was a gifted facilitator of personal development and leadership development workshops. His own life story involved overcoming tremendously difficult circumstances from the day he was born, to become the remarkable human being that he was. He died of cancer in his absolute prime on Friday 13th May 2011.

We worked closely together in the personal development arena. Indeed, the focus of our life together was what we could create together in this world. I remember shortly after we met picking up Dan Millman's book The Life You Were Born to Live and looking at what the numerology of my relationship with Doug entailed. It was all about the work we could do together, creating something together, helping others together. And indeed that is a big part of what our relationship was about.

Doug had talked for several years about wanting to write a book setting out the concepts underlying his teaching and illustrating its impact on his own life as an inspiration to others. He didn't get that book written before he died, so I am picking up the baton. I'll use what I know of his story, along with my own, to illustrate the concepts. It is important to me (and to Doug) that this book is about real life. Our stories will help to bring life and meaning to what we have to share. As Doug used to say:

"This is not a philosophy class."

It's about the real world. About living life at a higher level and making a difference in, and with, our lives every day.

I started putting down the outline for this book on, what would have been, Doug's 59th birthday. It seemed like the perfect day to finally get this project underway. The book he had wanted to write himself and yet seemed reluctant to get started. What was he reticent about? Perhaps of revealing more of his story to the world. Masterful as he was, he was still growing and taking his own life to his next level. To him personal growth and development was a lifetime journey. And that is something he demonstrated to the very end... not a philosophy, but a way of being that he demonstrated to his last breath.

And I find myself feeling a sense of urgency now to get this written. If I am old enough to have had a husband who would be 59 today, that means I am getting on myself now too! Better press on with writing this book. Telling Doug's story, our story. Spreading the power of what we learned and applied in our lives and what we taught others.

And so, with enormous gratitude to all the wise teachers who have brought my life to this place, but most especially to Doug, let's begin.

Chapter 1: In the Beginning

Our Roots

I was born Claire Safford in Wakefield, Yorkshire in the north of England at the end of 1959. That puts me firmly in the baby boomer generation.

I grew up in a middle class family in a small town in Yorkshire with my brother and sister. In some ways we were a very ordinary family, in others not so. My father was a power station engineer. He had come from a working class background in Hull. He left school at 15 to start work and quickly rose to the top of his field. At the age of 19 he was in charge of the control room at the power station. My mother was a teacher. Unusually for the time, she went back to work once the three of us were at school.

By the age of 16, I had decided that I wanted a career rather than children, and, that I didn't feel I could do justice to either if I tried to do both. I also remember thinking that I didn't want to get landed trying to bring up kids on my own like my mother had. Another unusual aspect of my upbringing... at that time it was rare for people to separate and/or divorce. My parents split up when I was 12. I didn't know anyone else in school whose parents were not together. Sadly, an aspect of society that has changed dramatically!

The formula for success that I was taught, at home and at school, was work hard at getting a good education. From there you will be able to get a good job and then you will be comfortably taken care of for the rest of your life, if you keep working hard. How the world has changed!

I followed the formula. I got a Bachelor's degree and then a Master's degree in Economics and Statistics/Econometrics. I got a job with prospects, and that suited my aptitudes. I started work in London with a global insurance broker in the risk management consulting subsidiary. Continuing to apply the formula, I worked hard to climb the corporate ladder.

On the personal side, I was in a stable and comfortable relationship with a kind and gentle man who was also following the same formula.

In 1990, at the age of 30, I was given the opportunity to transfer to the Toronto office in Canada. Serendipitously, my partner also got a job transfer to Toronto at the same time... how amazing is that? We jumped at the opportunity, sold up in the UK and continued to apply the formula.

We worked hard, we carried on climbing the corporate ladder, we bought a house, we drove late model cars, we took interesting holidays around the world as well as trips to the UK to visit family, and we had a good circle of people to socialize with. I travelled throughout North America for business. I was also in Zurich and Bermuda regularly. I had a fancy title and the commensurate salary and perks.

What a life! OK I was exhausted all the time, caught colds all winter, had no energy left for anything outside of work and the socializing it required, was stressed out and feeling taken advantage of... but I was living the high life according to the formula.

By 1994, I was beginning to hear a little voice in my head saying "Is this it? Is this all there is to life? Working 60-70 hour weeks for what?" I started to feel like there was something missing. An emptiness. As though my life was a wonderful façade on the outside, but there was nothing of substance that I valued on the inside. I heard that small voice saying, "What difference are you making on the planet even though you are working so hard and giving so much time and energy to your work?" And then, loudly and determinedly, one day I heard the voice saying, "There has to be a better way to live my life."

That was the start of my journey to a Full Spectrum Life and living life at a higher level. It was that thought which lead me to start doing personal development work myself and ultimately to assisting others in their own personal development. In July 1994, on the recommendation of a trusted friend, I attended a weekend experiential workshop that changed my life. At the end of the weekend I knew in my heart that, yes, there was a better way to live my life and that I had the power to change my life experience and live life at a higher level.

Jim Quinn's Lifestream Basic, is where the seeds were planted for what my life has become. A year later I met Doug Cameron and the stage was set for my world to change direction dramatically.

Contrast my relatively normal start in life with the hand that Doug was dealt. He was born Nicholas Wordley in Oshawa, just outside Toronto, Canada. His mother, a young single woman, gave him up for adoption at birth, as was the normal practice in those circumstances back in 1954.

A local couple, who already had a five year old daughter of their own, adopted baby Nicholas. They renamed him Douglas Andrew Cameron. When he was just three years old, his first adoptive mother died and the torment of his early days began in earnest.

Two years before he died, Doug wrote about his early life with the intention of including it in his book. I knew he had been writing, but had never seen it until I was searching for something in his computer files a few weeks ago. So I'll let him tell you that part of the story in his own words. He wrote it in the third person, but most certainly it is his story.

In His Own Words: Doug Cameron
(Born Nicholas Wordley)

Nicholas Wordley came into this world in an adventurous, if somewhat unfortunate way. The story of his journey is personal, profound, difficult, painful, joyful, challenging, stressful, overwhelming, small, pathetic, and ultimately, a story of breakthrough to a new and profoundly grateful self.

In later life, Nicholas would develop a purpose and passion in life: to guide, teach, lead and otherwise facilitate people on how to break through self-limiting beliefs and self-defeating behaviours. To create systems and methodologies that enable them to create a life of their choosing. To discover, or re-discover their purpose, their personal power, and their passion in life. To develop a truly meaningful life purpose. To be less driven by destructive emotions and negative paradigms, and to be more resourceful, more creative, more resilient and more determined to take charge of the quality of their own lives.

So before getting to all of that, the intention in telling Nicholas' story is to build, if you will, some 'street cred'. His history and background have given him some unique perspectives on life. His personal story, combined with the skills he has acquired over many years, and a powerful, intuitive understanding of human nature, have equipped him to uniquely show others a pathway for them to experience the results of change in their lives.

Nicholas was born in 1954 to a young, unwed mother. The social norms of the day dictated that he be put up for adoption, which he promptly was. Nicholas was adopted by a kind, caring, and loving young couple. They were both terrified and excited in equal measure at this very young, healthy baby boy coming into their lives. They already had one young daughter, born five years previously.

Had the rest of his early life been somewhat less brutal and less traumatic, he likely would have been eternally grateful for this happy event. As such was not the case, he has always had a very hard time with forgiving his birth mother for giving him up. For many years, his self-talk around this was, "I would rather live in the gutter with my 'real' mother," than live in the relatively comfortable, middle class circumstances that he did actually grow up in.

As the twists of fate would have it, Nicholas' first adopted mother died when he was three years old. This was the ultimate maternal abandonment in his young life. He never knew what she died of. In his family of the time, it was never spoken of, or referred to in any way. What that event did for him, was to set up a state of depression, ranging from severe to clinical, which he maintained for the rest of his life. In the late 1950's there was no child therapy, or any services where a child could process or release the terrible sense of bewilderment, abandonment, and isolation, that the death of a parent can create for a young child. If there were some who did recognize such a need, it was never spoken of and no one dared interfere in another family's private grief. A result of this is that he has suffered depression, sometimes severe, at times clinical, since he was 3 years old.

Upon his first adopted mother's death, his adopted father took the first, and probably the most sensible, refuge that was offered. They moved into Nicholas' adopted grandparents' house. In their own grief and confusion, they, and the rest of the family, were just trying to cope with this terrible tragedy, do their best, and do what was right.

Having lived with his adopted grandparents for about a year, Nicholas' adopted father re-married. He had met and married a dynamic young woman who was accomplished in the diplomatic service. She had worked in various positions for the Canadian government. During World War II she worked in the Australian Embassy in Washington D.C. Now in her late 30's, she agreed to take Nicholas' father as her husband along with his two children. So, at this point in his life, Nicholas is four years old and has had four different mothers – his birth mother, his first adopted mother, his adopted grandmother, and his second adopted mother.

Let me make a side note here: Nicholas has an older sister and a younger brother. They are only mentioned here for family circle completeness. There is no intention of telling their story here. The reference is for when it is integral to Nicholas' own story. As of this writing, they are both alive and can tell their own story, should they so choose. Both of Nicholas' adopted parents have passed and they will be referenced as a more central part of his experience.

The woman Nicholas' father married brought her own, well developed amalgam of grief and resentment into the struggling young family. Born in 1920, she had come from a farm family where alcoholism and violence were the norm. In 1943 she had *married a young Canadian fighter pilot. This dashing and handsome young man was shot down and killed over Germany, less than one month after they were married.*

So, now Nicholas is being raised by two adopted parents, widow and widower, both tragically dealt a foul hand by life's circumstances. Good, decent people consumed by anger, fear, guilt and resentment. However, this was the late 1950's/early 1960's. Middle class respectability was the order of the day. Anything dark, destructive, dysfunctional, or 'not normal' was never mentioned; skeletons only to be swept into very tightly closed closets.

When he was six years old Nicholas' family moved from a small city to a big city. Of course being six, he was pretty much bewildered by this experience. He was sent here and there, told to do this and that, and he pretty much complied with the program he was given. By the time Nicholas was seven, he had settled in and had several neighborhood friends. One of his young friends lived six houses away up the street. He had an older brother who, at the time, was sixteen.

Now to a seven year old, a sixteen year old is a big person. A person of authority, someone to be followed, someone who was O.K. Not long after he had acclimated to this friend's family, Nicholas would often go to their house to play. It was not long after he had started to play there, that they would often go up to his older brother's room to play. They would wrestle and have tickle fights, laugh and giggle. It wasn't long before all of their clothes had come off and the tickling went to new, unusual, and pleasurable sensations. The older brother was very good at this.

The sexual molestation went on for many months. Eventually something was discovered by parents and it came to an end. As is well known by anyone who has been victimized by a sexual abuser, and as is well documented in the mental health profession, the effects of even one incident of sexual molestation of a child can have dramatic negative effects on that person for a lifetime. Nicholas' exposure to incidents of abuse were multiple, and over an extended period of time.

So by now Nicholas is more than a little confused about life, about relationships, about who or what he is and is not. Having had four different mothers by the age of four, one of whom died when he was three, Nicholas is being raised by well meaning, but deeply scarred and damaged 'parents', and, he is being sexually abused.

But wait! He is still only seven. There is more to come. Because he was more than a little confused about ... see above, and because there was no treatment or therapy of any kind for children, Nicholas began to act out in a variety of ways in what might be described as difficult, aberrant, truant. He would steal things, he would find ways to avoid school and he would get into minor scrapes and bits of trouble. Nothing serious, just the garden variety things that now are referred to as a child 'being an individual', or 'expressing his uniqueness'.

However, Nicholas was being raised by an adopted father who was a very respectable man. A pillar of the community. An honorable and a decent man. A man with military service who had fought in World War II. A strict disciplinarian who believed he was to be obeyed at all times. He never questioned authority. Children never questioned authority. Children were to be seen and not heard.

So with all the confusion and turmoil in Nicholas, and the resultant acting out, combined with his adopted father's inability, or unwillingness, to attempt to discover what was really going on with

Nicholas, his father believed that his only option was the severest of disciplinary measures. The result was that Nicholas was severely beaten and whipped with a leather belt on numerous occasions for a period of several years. While the bruises, welts, and physical pain were excruciating, the psychological and emotional trauma was devastating to the core of Nicholas' being. Now any sense of 'self' for him was shattered beyond any recognition.

Abandoned, abused, beaten and battered, Nicholas was now 10! He was still being raised by two well-meaning but tragically confused people. He was physically provided for. They had a nice house, all the clothes, food, and accessories of normal middle class life. They even had a summer cottage up north where they spent all of their summers. But the "I", the sense of self, the "personhood" of Nicholas was emotionally barren, a scorched earth. He had no sense of feeling love for or from his parents. He didn't have any sense of emotion for anyone or anything. It's not that he didn't have any emotions, it is more that his emotions had become a toxic stew of anger, rage, fear; out-of-control drivers on a wild no-rules demolition derby.

Now layer over this the clear expectation that he was still a "good boy". They were, after all, still a respectable middle class family. With limited or no options to externalize or process his emotions, his only option, from his point of view, was to turn completely inward.

Nicholas became severely introverted. Socially mummified. He locked himself into an internally created prison. As far as the world was concerned, his only choice was to circle his wagons, defend himself at all costs. He created an internal place where no one was getting in and he wasn't coming out.

Nicholas remembers very clearly an incident that occurred years later. It turned out to be the most profound moment he was to have in all of the therapy he was to engage in over many years. He was telling the therapist (who was brilliant and one of the best he had ever been to), that "I know they (my adopted parents) must have loved me (because that's what parents do, isn't it?), but I never actually felt loved." The therapist looked at him and said, "Perhaps you weren't loved by your parents." Nicholas distinctly remembers feeling a deep chill come over his whole body. That comment shot through his heart like a bolt of solid ice. He had been desperately clinging to the belief that he must have been loved by his adopted parents (because all children are loved by their parents, aren't they?) In that moment, in that room, with that very talented and compassionate healer, Nicholas' whole belief system around his love relationship with his parents shattered.

For the first time in his life he had to acknowledge, and then accept, that he probably wasn't loved by his adopted parents. At least not in any conventional, or generally accepted sense of what maternal, and paternal, love means. Whilst this was the singularly most painful and devastating moment of realization in his recovery process, it was also a new plateau from which he could now begin to climb to a higher level of renewal and regeneration of himself into, what might be loosely referred to as, a functioning human being.

When he was 11, his parents enrolled Nicholas in a very fine and reputable Canadian military cadet organization. Oddly, Nicholas actually did quite well there and began to advance through the ranks. There was only one major problem here. The senior cadet in the corps was the first person to introduce Nicholas to drugs. He invited Nicholas over to his house one evening with one of the other cadets. They went up to this boy's room and he brought out the marijuana. Nicholas, who was 13 at the time, had no idea what this was. Wanting to be one of the gang, he gladly joined in and started on what would become a twenty plus year odyssey of drug addiction and alcoholism.

No matter which way he turned in life, the people, events and circumstances in Nicholas' life always seemed to turn to the negative, the destructive, the dysfunctional and the toxic. Was he pre-disposed or pre-determined to this path? Was his life some kind of karmic retribution for past evil deeds? If you believe in the idea of Karma, then he must have been some kind of bad-assed, mean and dastardly son-of-a-bitch in a previous life. Because it seems like he was destined to take some kind of nasty Karmic shit-kicking this time around. Of course, from the other side, if you really understand the Law of Karma, then, despite all of the challenges he faced in his early life, this current life may actually be a step up from a previous life that was really painful! Hot Dog! What an opportunity to be grateful for pain and suffering!

Be that as it may, getting back to his story, the next three or four years grew increasingly intolerable in terms of his relationship with his adopted father. This was the late 1960's, early 70's and the hippies, and the Beatles, were all the rage. Tune in, turn on, drop out was the order of the day. His father and he were both increasingly barricaded in their two very distant worlds. There was a huge void between them and neither one of them was willing or able to bridge the chasm. At the age of 15, Nicholas quit school and left home. He became one of the proverbial street kids, the kind you read about in the media. He very quickly found Yorkville, Rochdale, Kensington Market and the Annex areas in Toronto.

He hung out, hustling for money and drugs. You do know what young teenage boys living on the streets, do for money and drugs, don't you? He drifted around, got himself into all manner of dark and dangerous places. He did a lot of drugs, including injecting hard drugs. He was either really resourceful, or really lucky. He managed to get himself out, for the most part, of those dark and dangerous places. Many did not. Some suffered much more physical and sexual abuse at the hands of others. Some came to their own end either from despair or from drug deluded acts that ended in permanent physical or mental disability, or in their death.

By age 17, Nicholas was out on the highway, hitchhiking out west to British Columbia. The next couple of years were actually quite good and contain some of the best and fondest memories of his life to that point. He spent most of that time living in the mountain regions in southern B.C. It was really a wonderful, wild time. Where he lived there was a large community of hippies, draft dodgers (this was the early 70's), runaway kids and all kinds of travelling folks from all over. They lived in tents and teepees, some had log cabins. They mostly smoked a lot of pot, hung out, made love, and enjoyed the good life, such as it was. This was the ultimate escape from the horror and tragedy of the early life of Nicholas Wordley.

Picking Up Where Doug Left Off

This is where Doug's writing finished. However, there is a whole other story still to tell to bring him to the point of discovering the work that was to become his passion, his gift to the world and a large part of the basis for this book. Let me fill in that part of the story, as I know it, from what he told me of his life before I met him.

We left him living in a teepee in Southern BC, Canada at the age of 17. He did casual work in sawmills and fruit picking in the orchards of the Okanagan Valley. At the age of 18 he lied about his age (you had to be 19) and got a job as a brakeman on the railway running out of Revelstoke. He used to describe to me the joy of sitting on the train rumbling through the glorious mountain scenery of the Canadian Rockies.

This is where the chronology gets a little confusing. He lived in Vancouver and in Sooke on Vancouver Island. He spent some time in Winnipeg working in a carpet store and then was sent to Edmonton to open up a new location for the carpet company. He traveled to and from Toronto a couple of times, deciding to return there to live when he was 23. He did eventually re-establish contact with his adopted family.

He applied to do an undergraduate degree at York University in Toronto as a mature student. That meant he had to wait another year until he was 24 to qualify. So he started working in bars and restaurants until he could start his course full time.

He graduated with a degree in Economics and started into the hospitality industry in earnest. He worked in kitchens, he waited table, he ran bars and he managed restaurants. He had his own catering company servicing an up market Toronto clientele. He was a natural with anything to do with food.

He worked as an assistant editor on a series of the Canadian TV show Street Legal. He assisted a well-known Canadian film director to write and market a screenplay in Hollywood. The screenplay was purchased by Mel Gibson and was released as

The Man Without a Face. Film and theatre was one of his interests throughout his life. He also worked in real estate in Toronto.

In 1982, at the age of 27, he met and fell in love with a beautiful young woman. The feeling was mutual and they quickly married. In August 1983 he was blessed with the birth of his son. The photographs from that time show how happy and delighted Doug was with his beautiful wife and their baby boy. Perhaps his life had finally turned a corner!

But that respite was not to last long for Doug. A few months after his son was born, Doug's wife was persuaded by her parents to return with the baby to their home in Germany. A long, frustrating and, ultimately, fruitless time trying to get access to his son ensued. A time during which Doug sank deeper into the abyss of depression and alcoholism. He began to think that perhaps this was his lot in life. Perhaps this pain, suffering and despair was all he could expect from life.

It was 1987 when he first encountered the work of the late Jim Quinn. His real estate partner and great friend got him into the Lifestream Basic weekend. Doug used to describe how finally, that weekend, he saw a glimmer of hope. He had his last drink a year later in April 1988.

He didn't do it alone though. Alcoholics Anonymous proved to be a critical factor in his recovery, as with so many other addicts around the globe. The same friend supported him in his journey through AA, ultimately becoming his sponsor. As is often the case, Doug had several goes at AA before he "got it". Then the light came on and he began to understand the depth of the path he was embarking on. Between Lifestream and AA,

Doug had a support network and the tools to change his life. If you are familiar with AA's 12 Steps and 12 Traditions you will see them reflected in various parts of this book.

It took years of therapy, counselling, personal development and sheer will power for him to achieve the level of freedom from his past that he did achieve. It started with his great friend introducing him to Jim Quinn and the AA programme.

Doug and I met in 1995 at a Jim Quinn seminar. Doug was being trained by Jim to facilitate. I was a volunteer team leader. We married in 1997. Our time together involved many adventures, big and small, personal and professional. Armed with the tools and understanding that are set out in this book we were able to make a happy life together, accepting each other for who each of us was and bringing out the best in each other.

Chapter 2: Getting Value from this Book

There is quite a contrast between Doug's and my background. Yet we both changed our lives for the better as a result of applying the same tools, techniques and principles that you are going to learn in this book. It is important for you to realize that, whatever your circumstances, the teaching underlying this book can help you to live life at a higher level, to live a Full Spectrum Life. The principles apply universally. Jim Quinn used to say,

"This work is about good people becoming even better."

No matter how well, or badly, life is working for you just now, there is always the opportunity to make life work even better.

The tools, techniques and principles in this book can help you to manage - no master - stress, attract more positive people into your life, use higher level thinking to bring balance to your life, have more fun in life and treat yourself and others with greater kindness and respect and to experience life with more enthusiasm.

We spend years of our life, and substantial amounts of money, going through traditional education. At the end of it we may have a highly developed intellectual capability, but our personal and interpersonal skills and capabilities are often not well developed. Despite all the technology that pervades our lives, relationships are still fundamental to our health, happiness and success in both our professional and personal lives. To live a

Full Spectrum Life we need to spend some time and effort learning skills in all four pillars.

We also need to start to look at things a little differently. How we experience the world depends crucially on how we perceive the world. You can get to this truth from numerous angles, whether that be quantum physics, Buddhist teachings, many of the human potential writers and teachers or your own observation.

It is not always easy to change the way we view ourselves and the world around us. First of all we need to become aware of how we perceive our world. That means looking deeply behind what is going on at the surface for us.

There are three ways that you can read this book: you can always agree with what is written, you can always disagree and dismiss or you can pause and look deeper at your life. Of course, the latter is the effective way to get value from this book.

This book isn't about being right or wrong. It isn't about being told what to do. It's about providing some perspectives, some tools and techniques that may give you new insights into how you are living your life and how you can make your life work better – whatever that means for you.

As you read, I will bet that, at some point, you are going to find yourself thinking "That's it! If only so and so realized that and changed the way they deal with me." At those moments, it is critical that you remember something Doug used to say:

"There are only two ways your life will
improve: either the rest of the world changes,
or you change. Which has the greatest
probability of success?"

Some of what you read here may be new and challenging. Some may be familiar. Whatever the case, pause and look deeper – most especially around the concepts that are familiar. It is easy to skim, and miss an important insight, if you are reading with an attitude of "Oh, I know this. I've heard it before." Keep pausing and looking deeper. Perhaps now is the right time for you to take that particular concept to a whole new level in your life. There are layers within layers to everything you are going to come across in this book.

Resistance and avoidance are a natural reaction to change. "I know this" is a pretty common avoidance tactic. Before you go on reading, give yourself a moment to think about the ways you avoid so that you are prepared, if that should happen as you read on.

Keep a notebook with you as you read this book and journal your insights, thoughts and responses. They will be valuable to you as you move forward with living your life at a higher level. The very act of writing them out causes shifts. And journaling as you read is a sure fire way to help you to pause and look deeper.

Chapter 3: Living Life at a Higher Level

The subtleties of words are important. The word used is "higher", a relative term. It is not "high", which is an absolute term. If we used the word "high" it would suggest that there is some "correct" level to achieve which, once achieved, is the end of the journey. Achieve that "high" level and you have made it. No more growth necessary. Nowhere else to go.

But that is not what life is about. You have heard the phrases, "Life is a journey." Or, "It's not about the final destination; it's about how we get there." Clichéd as they might sound, they are true! We all face the same final destination… we are all going to die one day. Until that day, there are infinite possibilities for us to choose as we head towards our last day.

Doug's last 11 months of life were such an example of continuing to live life at a higher and higher level even as life was slipping away from him. We left his story at the point of him finding hope at Jim Quinn's Lifestream weekend, followed a year later by him taking his last drink. Fast forward 22 years. It is the summer of 2010. Having had nose bleeds on and off for a few months, one day he had one that he just couldn't stop. So off he went to the walk in clinic and then down to the hospital, where they had better equipment to get a look at what was going on.

Even more specialized equipment was required and so an appointment with an ENT consultant followed the next day. That resulted in an immediate CAT scan of his upper sinuses. Clearly, something was amiss. Yet Doug calmly and courageously took it all in his stride. Doug spent July 1st 2010, Canada Day, a day of celebration, fun and picnics, at the hospital having a biopsy of a "mass" in his upper sinus area. Three days later we sat together in the consultant's office to hear the diagnosis. It was a rare cancer of the olfactory nerve. Still Doug remained calm and composed, accepting and courageous.

Doug recovered quickly from the surgery to remove the tumour and just six weeks later was back giving his gift to the world by facilitating a Full Spectrum Leadership breakthrough weekend workshop. He seemed more "on", more alive, more connected than ever. He was living life at an even higher level with every intention of making his impact felt in every aspect of his life.

At the beginning of March 2011, Doug facilitated a five day intensive residential leadership programme for a group of people committed to making themselves and the world better. A week after finishing that, he couldn't make his own mind up what he wanted to eat off a menu. A few days later, he didn't even know what city he was in. Where five months previously there was no sign of any cancer, now there was a large cancerous tumour in his brain. Still he remained calm and peaceful as his mental and physical faculties started to ebb away.

Even as he lay in a hospice bed through the last six weeks of his life, he was still setting an example for all those around him. The cancer in his brain prevented him from processing information in such a way as to be able to answer any more than the occasional yes or no. He was not able to get out of bed unaided or walk. Yet he radiated peace, compassion and courage to everyone who came into contact with him.

Nurses at the hospice who had spent 20 plus years in end of life care told me they had never experienced anyone living their last days like Doug did. To his last breath, his journey was about living his life at a higher and higher level radiating love and compassion.

Do you think I did some growing and some moving of my life to a higher level through that experience too? You bet I did. What I have written here is a tiny snapshot of all that happened during that time. Just enough to illustrate the point.

When we are living life at a higher level it means that we are becoming more professional at life. We are becoming more and more who we *really* are. We are manifesting on the outside more and more of the substance and values we have on the inside. Who we really are, and who the world sees are in greater and greater alignment. In other words, we are living in increasing integrity and authenticity.

There is no right or wrong level to be at. As Abraham-Hicks says "I am where I am and that's OK." The important thing is to be moving towards living life at a *higher* level and a higher level and a higher level...

There are two fundamental principles that underpin our ability to live a Full Spectrum Life that is moving to higher and higher levels. Let's take a look.

The Commitment Principle:

> *My life works in direct proportion to the*
> *commitments I make and keep...*
> *Including those I make to myself.*

There is so much in this short phrase! Isn't life all about being committed? How often do you *try* to achieve something? Or you tell yourself you *might* do it one day? Or you *think* you will have a go at something? Have you ever really *committed* to something? Are the results different?

Then of course it is not just about making a commitment but *keeping* it. A commitment made but not kept is just a pipe dream, wishful thinking.

The keeping part of The Commitment Principle is all about action. Without action there is nothing. Action is not necessarily "doing" though. For example, it might be a thought pattern, changing an emotional response, spending time incubating an idea or response.

Are you really good at keeping commitments you make to other people at the expense of your own desires and plans? What would your life feel like if you were as good at making and keeping commitments to yourself as you are with commitment to others?

Before I learned about and understood The Commitment Principle, I was really good at making and keeping all kinds of commitments to others, mostly around my job. But I had actually stopped making commitments to things outside of work, including myself, because there always seemed to be something that needed my commitment at work. And, of course, when you are the one who will always be counted on to get stuff done at work no matter what, then you are the one who always gets called upon. The overwhelming domination of work became a self-fulfilling feedback loop.

When I first heard The Commitment Principle I remember thinking, "I don't want more commitment, I want less. I want freedom!" The truth of this principle sank in when I did start making and keeping commitments to myself. I began to feel freer. I began to feel less shackled. Perhaps the ultimate commitment I made was to marry Doug and in doing so I felt freer than I could ever remember being.

At work, I remember the exhilaration, confidence and centeredness I felt the first time I said "No. I am sorry I cannot do that. I have another commitment." That commitment was that I should get some rest and relaxation that weekend no matter what anyone at the office asked me to come in to do.

Keeping a commitment is so much easier if you set up accountability at the same time. Have you ever experienced how different a commitment is when you have told someone about what you are planning compared to if you just keep it to yourself? The most successful people have coaches and mentors to provide a sounding board, a different perspective and a point of accountability.

The Commitment Principle is one of those powerful truths that unveil deeper and deeper layers as you bring it further into your daily life. Try it. Make commitment to your life, your values, your integrity, your passion, your contribution a centerpiece to the way you conduct yourself every day. And set up an accountability system. Find a mentor, a coach, someone who will not buy into your excuses.

The Responsibility Principle:

I, and I alone, am 100% responsible for the
quality of my entire life experience.

Now The Responsibility Principle often causes some resistance and debate. The resistance usually sounds something like this, "How can I be responsible for being abused?" Or, "How can I be responsible for my wife cheating on me?" Or, "How can I be responsible for being injured in that car crash?" Or, "How can I be responsible for my husband dying?" You get the idea.

There are schools of thought that say yes you are responsible because everything that shows up in your life you have attracted, whether consciously or subconsciously. This is *NOT* what The Responsibility Principle is about.

There is a critical distinction to make which takes away those resistance arguments and the need for belief in The Law of Attraction. Here is the distinction:

The Responsibility Principle is about
Life Experience NOT Life Circumstances.

The resistance all comes when we get into a debate over who is responsible for our life circumstances. As Doug used to say, circumstances are just circumstances.

We experience life through the way we think, the way we feel and the way we behave. Therefore, our life experience has nothing to do with circumstances and everything to do with how we respond to those circumstances in the way we think, feel and behave.

And who is responsible for the way you think, the way you feel and the way you behave. It's you, and you alone!

Let's take a couple of classic examples:

- Many child abusers were themselves abused. However, not every child who is abused becomes an abuser. The opposite can happen. Often those working to protect children from abuse were themselves abused. The abuse is a circumstance. The life experience is determined by how the abused responds with thoughts, feelings and behaviours.

- Many alcoholics were brought up by alcoholic parents. However not every child of an alcoholic becomes an alcoholic. Some choose to avoid alcohol consumption all together. Again the alcoholic parent is a circumstance. The life experience is determined by the choice of the way we think, feel and behave in the circumstance.

And a third example from my own experience. Back in the mid 1990's I had a friend who was HIV positive. He was a gay man who, of course in that community, knew many others living with HIV and dying of AIDS. His choice as to his life experience from that circumstance was to recklessly live his life in full party-mode... alcohol, drugs, fast cars, clubs. It was as though he was determined to make an early death a self-fulfilling prophecy.

Contrast that with someone I met in 2005. A middle aged woman who had been HIV positive for 25 years. She did not know she was carrying the virus until 5 years after contracting it when her 9 month old baby daughter died of AIDS. The death of a child can crush a parent. Death from an illness that you know you have passed to the baby must be even harder to bear. However, instead of being crushed by this circumstance, she allowed it to lift her into becoming an inspirational speaker for young people and an activist for those living with HIV.

So the bottom line on The Responsibility Principle is that, whilst I may be dealing with a difficult life circumstance, I can take charge of how I experience that circumstance by choosing my thoughts, feelings and behaviours in such a way as to move me towards living life at a higher level, rather than spiraling down to a lower level. Simple but not necessarily easy.

The key to remember is that we ALWAYS have a CHOICE as to the thoughts, feelings and behaviours we engage. It takes discipline and practice to gradually make more choices that take us to living life at a higher level, and to make those choices with greater speed. Living by choice, rather than by living my knee jerk reaction, is a necessary result of living by The Responsibility Principle.

Perhaps one of the most extreme examples and powerful proponents of The Responsibility Principle is Viktor Frankl. Born in Vienna in 1905, Frankl was a neurologist and a psychiatrist. He was also Jewish. He spent three years from 1942 to 1945 imprisoned in Nazi concentration camps. There, he observed those around him and he observed himself. He became aware of what he subsequently referred to as "the last of the human freedoms". Whilst the prison guards controlled every aspect of his external existence, they could not control what went on in his mind. He recognized that he, and every one of the other prisoners, had the choice as to how he responded to those desperate, unthinkable circumstances. His survival and ability to go on after his liberation to contribute so greatly to his field, depended on that awareness and the mental discipline he was able to apply during his terrible imprisonment. The difference between Frankl and most others in the camps, was that he was aware of this opportunity to choose his experience within the circumstance, most were not. Most were living in fear-based reactionism experiencing horrendous suffering.

After his liberation, Frankl went on to develop his observations and experiences into a branch of psychiatry he named Logotherapy. His most famous book, Man's Search for Meaning, tells of his time in the camps and sets out his insights as described by Logotherapy.

What makes human beings different from other animal species is that we have free will; we can choose how we respond to a given set of circumstances.

In his book The 7 Habits of Highly Effective People, Stephen Covey uses a different spelling of the word responsibility to make this point so clearly. Responsibility becomes "response-ability", i.e. the ability to respond rather than react.

When we 'get' this, when we really start to get that we are 100% responsible for the quality of our own life experience, then life changes. I vividly remember the moment I got it.

It was a few months after I had attended a five day residential personal development workshop at a retreat centre outside of Toronto, Canada. Afterwards, I remembered the facilitator saying that the impacts and insights from the workshop would not all happen during the week itself. Rather, that what we experienced at the workshop would unfold for us over weeks, months and perhaps years in the future.

So there I was, weeks after the workshop and the integration follow up was finished. It was a grey Saturday morning. I woke up and went into the bathroom to splash some water on my face and clean my teeth before heading downstairs. I was quite sleepy. I looked at myself in the mirror and from the sleepiness was hit by a moment of astounding clarity and alertness. I heard my inner voice saying loud and clear "This is it. No more excuses. I, and I alone, am 100% responsible for my entire life experience." I felt as though I had been hit by a 2 by 4 around the head. From that moment my life changed.

At first, more often than not, you will probably be using The Responsibility Principle to change an unpleasant experience you are having as a result of reacting to a circumstance. However, armed with The Responsibility Principle, along with other tools and techniques you will learn as we progress through the book, you now know that, no matter what, you can always choose to change the quality of your life experience as it unfolds.

Eventually, you won't be using The Responsibility Principle to change unpleasant experiences. Rather, you will be avoiding unpleasant experiences by making your choice as to how you think, feel and behave in a circumstance up front before the reaction leading to unpleasant experience kicks in.

Just pause for a moment now and contemplate the power of what you have just read. Imagine experiencing your life from the point of view of your choice of thoughts, feelings and behaviours at every moment, no matter what.

How are you feeling about that? Jim Quinn used to say that the biggest fear that people have is of taking charge of the quality of their own life. Are you feeling fearful? Are you feeling empowered? Are you feeling excited? This would be a really good time to make some notes in your journal!

Chapter 4: Four Pillars of a Full Spectrum Life

So far, we have explored two overarching principles that provide a framework for living life at a higher level. They are the two guiding lights that help to keep us on course as we move through life. When The Commitment Principle and The Responsibility Principle are foremost in our minds, we have a much greater possibility of having a positive life experience and achieving our desire of living a Full Spectrum Life at a higher and higher level.

Like any concept, the practical implementation can take different forms. Your application of the principles will be uniquely yours. However, it is useful to look at some of the practical 'how to's' associated with these overarching principles. The starting point is to answer the question, "What does living life at a higher level look like?" First of all, it is a *Full Spectrum Life*. And secondly, it is an *ever developing* Full Spectrum Life.

So what is a Full Spectrum Life? It is a life in which we are aware of, and focus attention on, developing all four of the fundamental aspects of ourselves as a human being: health (physical), wealth (mental), relationships (emotional) and contribution (spiritual). As we live life at a higher level, we are increasing the functionality and effectiveness of each of these four aspects and bringing them into balance with each other.

FOUR PILLARS

HEALTH, WEALTH, RELATIONSHIPS
AND CONTRIBUTION

I call the four aspects of a Full Spectrum Life the four pillars. Each pillar needs to be strong and balanced with the others in order to have a life that functions well and serves us and our purpose. If one pillar is weak or off balance, then the whole structure is weakened and may collapse.

I visualize these four pillars supporting each corner of the platform that is "life". It only takes one weak pillar and life is in danger of falling down. If one pillar is shorter than the others, life is in danger of crashing to the floor.

Having introduced the concept of the four pillars we can now further define a Full Spectrum Life and living life at a higher level. We are living a Full Spectrum Life when all four of our pillars are in balance i.e. the same height as each other. The platform they support that is our life is, therefore, on a stable footing. Living life at a higher level means that our four pillars are continuously growing taller, whilst maintaining their balance. Of course, it is not an exact science. Keeping the pillars in balance and growing is a juggling act, but it is, in essence, what life is about.

Here's a brief outline of each of the four pillars before we get into some detail on each of them.

- Health: Our physical nature. Health, energy, fitness, wellness. Does it affect all the other pillars?

- Wealth: Our mental nature. It is not just about money. Although, in today's world, the money equation has to work. Wealth includes career, wisdom, money, learning and fun.

- Relationships: Our emotional nature. Our lives are dominated by relationships. They may be life-long or only minutes in duration. When you dig deeply enough, most people's number one desire is to make their relationships better.

- Contribution: Our spiritual nature. It is about our self-esteem, self-love and self-worth. Our dreams and aspirations. And how it all feeds into our sense of contribution and purpose.

HEALTH

Pillar #1: Health

Health represents our physical nature. If our physical health gets out of balance it affects every other aspect of life. If you take a look in a book store you will find shelves and shelves full of books about health and wellness. Obviously, I can only scratch the surface in this discussion of the health pillar. So here are some questions to get you thinking, and journaling!

1. What lifestyle choices do you need to change in order to strengthen your health pillar? For example, are you a smoker? Are you overweight? Do you burn the candle at both ends?

2. Are you knowledgeable and conscious of what you are putting into your body in the form of food? Do your food choices nourish you and serve you or are they destroying your energy and health?
3. How are the other parts of your life – work, family, social, hobbies and activities – affected by your health and energy status?
4. Do you rely on painkillers, alcohol or any other potentially harmful substance to get you through the day?

Take a few minutes to write down your thoughts on these questions in your notebook. It will be time well spent I promise.

My big health awakening came around nutrition. I was about 39. I was in reasonable shape. Never smoked. Didn't drink much alcohol. No coffee or tea. Reasonable weight for my height. Ate lots of vegetarian food and not much red meat. Very little fast food, but a fair bit of pre-prepared food because of the busy life style. Took some vitamins every day and dosed myself heavily when I got a cold. Despite good sleep habits and meditation my energy levels were low. I thought it was just deep seated exhaustion from the busy city lifestyle.

Long story short, I ended up going to a naturopath because I got fed up of my doctor just writing a prescription to mask some symptoms I was having rather than finding out the underlying cause and dealing with that.

The naturopath put me on a strict diet which required me to avoid a long list of foods and ingredients. Grocery shopping became a conscious and focused event as I read every label and started to understand what I had been putting into my body even in the supposedly reasonably healthy choices I had been making. All those "low fat" products loaded with sugar and gums for example. Sugar in all kinds of savoury dishes. And starting to see the long list of chemical ingredients in so many products. It was an eye opener!

Diet was not the only thing I worked on with the naturopath. We used homeopathic products and nutritional supplements along with diet in order to get my body back into balance. And it worked. The symptoms disappeared. But more significant was that gradually, as the months went by, my energy came back and the fog in my brain lifted.

I was on the path to learning about nutrition, supplements and being conscious of what I put into my body. It has ultimately lead me to helping people to put together personalized nutrition plans to support their health and wellness goals as part of what I do.

There's another aspect to our physical nature that is worth discussing here; that is the connection between physical touch and wellbeing.

The ancient Greeks had a couple of dozen words for love, each describing a different aspect of love. Eros is the word that describes the physical aspect of love. Love expressed through touch, through holding and cuddling. It has been shown that, for proper physical, mental and emotional development, babies need to be held and cuddled. If they are not, they don't grow, gain strength or develop mentally and emotionally. They literally fade away.

As adults, when we do not experience touch, if we are not held and cuddled, we die inside. This is a particular problem for older people. From personal observation, I see that as people become elderly, they often find themselves experiencing little or no physical touch.

How can we express this Eros love in a respectful and acceptable manner? The answer is by offering a hug! It is widely accepted that we need 8 hugs a day for maintenance and 12 hugs a day to be growing in our wellbeing. I challenge you to see if you can give 8 – 12 heart to heart hugs a day this week.

Before you do that though, there is an important aspect to consider. Some people have issues with being touched or hugged. It is important to respect that. So what do we do? Always ask permission to give someone a hug. Say, "May I give you a hug?"

This is important for two reasons. First and foremost it respects the other person's wishes as to whether they want a hug or not. Secondly, it protects you from rejection. The wording is important. "May I give you a hug?" You haven't asked for a hug from them. You have offered a hug to them. How do you think you would feel if you asked someone for a hug and they refused? You would undoubtedly feel rejected. If you offer a hug and they refuse, it's not you they have rejected; it is the hug, and ultimately themselves. You are protected from rejection.

So where are you at with your health pillar? What commitments do you need to make with respect to your health? There are so many choices we make relating to health: nutrition (food, drink and supplements), exercise, sleep, stress management, hugs, time outdoors, regular dental, eye and medical check-ups, being aware of what is going on in our bodies… the list goes on. What accountability system are you going to put in place to help you not just make health commitments, but also keep them?

WEALTH

Pillar #2: Wealth

Wealth represents our mental nature. It is a much bigger concept than just money. However, it does include the money equation. If the money equation is out of balance that too can affect every other aspect of life. In addition to money, the wealth pillar takes in career, learning, wisdom, prosperity (in the broadest sense of the word), as well as fun and recreation.

The money equation is very important to the options that we can have available to us in life. However, money alone does not make a strong wealth pillar. Without mental stimulation, fun and recreation our wealth pillar is not fully established.

When I first started down the path to a Full Spectrum Life, the money part of my wealth pillar was doing fine. I was working within what I now know is a formula that is deeply flawed, however the short term money equation was well taken care of. But my wealth pillar was not well developed because I just wasn't having fun. I did very little to relax, rejuvenate and re-create.

Our mental nature is such a powerful tool in our ability to create the life we want. A later chapter in the book is devoted to the mind. Suffice to say here that the human mind is truly remarkable. As with every other aspect of our nature, we have the power to choose how to use it. We can use it to create chaos in our life, or peace. We can use it to focus on the petty, or the inspirational. We can use it to crush ourselves with fear and guilt, or to lift ourselves up and transcend even the direst of circumstances.

Recreation is often a neglected aspect of wealth. Break the word down and you get re-creation. Recreation is what allows us to recharge, rejuvenate and let go. It allows us to re-create ourselves ready for the next task.

We need fun and celebration in our lives. In fact, in the next chapter, you will see that this is one of the five steps in the model of personal development. We need to pause and reflect on achievements. It is something I have to constantly keep in my awareness. Being a task driven individual, it is too easy for me to just plough on with the next task rather than taking a break to have some fun, celebrate and connect.

Again some questions to get you thinking, and journaling.

- Do you have the financial resources that you need and desire today and in the future? Will you ever be able to afford to retire? When you stop working, will your income be sufficient for you to enjoy a fulfilling retirement or just survive?
- Have you mentally stagnated or are you still curious and learning?
- How much fun are you having in life? When was your last adventure – big or small? Do you take time to celebrate and to rest, relax and re-create?

My wealth pillar is now much stronger than it was. There are two main contributory factors to that. The first is that I now have diversified sources of income, some of which is residual, i.e. the money continues to flow long after I have done the work.

And secondly, I now make time for fun and re-creation by applying the overarching concept of commitment.

The author and educator, Robert Kiyosaki's book The Cashflow Quadrant totally changed the way I look at how to generate income. What I learned in that book has enabled me to get to the position of having a diversified source of income, including some residual income.

What is residual income? It is income that continues after the work is done. For example an author writes a book and is then paid every time the book is sold in the future. The same with songwriters, they are paid when their songs are played. The life insurance agent gets commission each time the premium is paid on a policy.

When my husband was taken ill in the summer of 2010, I was able to stop virtually all my work activity in order to focus on helping him through his treatments. When he became incapacitated I was able to spend my time with him at the hospice rather than working. A few months after my husband's death, I had still not got back into work when my father was diagnosed with cancer too. I was able to spend my time helping to support my father through his illness and final days. For close to three years I put absolutely no effort into my source of residual income and yet I continued to be paid throughout that time.

The old formula of "get an education, get a good job, work hard and you will be looked after" is well and truly defunct. However, anyone can successfully create a residual income if you carefully choose the vehicle to use.

I have already written about how my life changed when I started applying The Commitment Principle to commitments I had made to myself. First of all I began to actually make commitments to take some time for rest, relaxation, fun and recreation. It was a long time since I had made those kinds of commitments to myself. Secondly, I started keeping those commitments. How I felt about my life changed dramatically. I also became more productive and effective with my work time. It was a win-win solution.

Where are you at with your wealth pillar? What do you need to learn about how the money equation works in today's world? Who are you going to learn from? What commitments do you need to make to yourself around work, fun, recreation and learning? How will you hold yourself accountable?

RELATIONSHIPS

Pillar #3: Relationships

Relationships represent our emotional nature. When you think about it, our lives are dominated by relationships. They may be life-long or literally just minutes in duration. But everywhere we go and everything we do involves relationships. Living a Full Spectrum Life means being skillful in our relationships.

Perhaps the most important relationship of all is usually the most neglected. That is the relationship with our self. The quality of all other relationships stems from the relationship we have with our self. If we don't trust and respect ourselves, have compassion for ourselves, how can we trust, love and respect others?

I recently met someone who has great difficulty in making a connection with people. He really wants to engage with people in all forms of relationship, yet his fears resulting from his past life experiences keep him cut off. As I got to know this man, my first impressions of him were that he was incredibly hard on himself and critical of himself. Then when I realized how disconnected he was and yet how much he wanted to engage with people, I saw that before he can connect with other people in an open, trusting and kind way he needs to connect with himself that way. He needs to trust, love and respect himself before he will be able to happily and successfully connect with others. This relationship with self is key to authentic and comfortable relationships with others.

Relationships provide the means for us to experience our emotions. If we are not fully engaged in relationships then we are not fully engaged in our emotional nature.

When I went to that weekend workshop back in 1994 there was a moment I will never forget. The facilitator was talking about emotions and relationships. Then he said something which hit me so hard! He said, *"John Doe/Jane Doe, born 1900, died 1925, buried 1975."* There it was. That was me. I felt that statement not in my head, not in my heart, but at a visceral level almost as if it went right into every cell in my body. At that moment I committed to coming back from the dead and living my life at a higher level.

If you look deeply enough, pretty much everyone has a real desire to improve one, or some, or all their relationships. It may be a family relationship, an intimate relationship, work colleagues, clients or self.

47

When we talk about relationships and our emotional nature, there is another Greek word for love that is helpful to distinguish: the word Philios. This refers to brotherly love, love of community, the love that exists between friends and fellow community members be that a club, a company or other affiliation.

Denis Waitley in his book The Psychology of Winning talks about the basic human need to feel as though they "belong". This is philios love. I remember when I read that book. It was at a time when I worked for a large global corporation with 100,000 employees around the world. However, I worked in a small, specialist subsidiary with a strong sense of belonging to a team. In fact, the six of us who made up the London office when I joined are still in touch and meet up from time to time today close to 30 years on. The parent company decided to remove our separate identity and submerge us into the global morass of the main business. I remember how lost I felt. I remember how it felt as though somehow I had lost my sense of who I was. I didn't really understand what was happening to me at the time. It wasn't until I read that passage in Denis Waitley's book that I realized what was going on for me. That fundamental human need to belong had been undermined.

When you continue to look deeply, you find that communication is fundamental to the quality of relationships. When I realized that, it was great news. Whilst relationships seem rather complex and mysterious, I knew that communication skills could be learned, practiced and improved. Logically then, so could relationships.

The way we communicate with ourselves impacts our relationship with our self and in turn our relationships with everyone else around us. Are you really hard on yourself? Do you put yourself down? Are you critical, angry, disapproving, disappointed, disrespectful, uncaring or indifferent to yourself? If you can learn to be kinder to yourself, you will find that the relationships outside of yourself will take on new, more meaningful dimensions.

Today we live in a world of email, texts, Facebook, Twitter and so on. In some ways we are more connected to other people than ever. And yet how many of those connections are real relationships? People that you could count on for support, advice and help. And how many of your connections could count on you?

Whether it is in your business and professional life or your personal activities, the quality of your relationships will determine your success and fulfillment. Wouldn't it be interesting if there was a way for the accountants to measure the quality of a business' relationships along with usual assets and liabilities? That would be a sure fire way of deciding where to invest!

Jim Rohn talks about the need to make careful choices about who we are associated with. Sometimes, because of history, we find ourselves connected to people who are detrimental to our life and the path we are on today. It is important to invest our time in relationships that serve us and our purpose, so that we can be the best that we can be. Thus, we are able to share the best of our self and our gifts with the world around us.

He says that it may be necessary to cut the ties to certain particularly toxic relationships. In less toxic situations it may be possible to manage the relationship in such a way as to limit exposure to the toxicity. For example, by choosing to limit the amount of time we spend with someone. Or, by dealing with them in short telephone conversations.

As a frightened and confused teenager, Doug's instincts told him that he needed to cut himself off from the toxicity of his adoptive parents. Even as an adult, with all the strength he had and the healing work that he went through, Doug chose to manage his exposure to them in order to avoid being sucked back into a toxic world.

To conclude this introduction to the relationship pillar, here are some key points in this vast and complex subject matter:

- We are not alive if we are not experiencing our emotional nature through relationships of all kinds.
- The quality of your relationship with your self is fundamental to the quality of your relationship with others.
- Communication is fundamental to the success of relationships, including the relationship with our self. Communication skills can be learned and developed.
- Philios love, brotherly love, the sense of belonging is an important human need.
- Relationships can be managed to ensure they are serving you in fulfilling your purpose and being the best you, you can be.

Take a few minutes now to journal and make some notes about the state of your relationships. Do you have a pool of real relationships not just virtual connections? How is your relationship with yourself? Do you need to make a commitment to further develop relationships in order to change the quality of your business or personal experience? Are you John or Jane Doe, born 1900, died 1925, buried 1975?

Pillar #4: Contribution

Contribution reflects the aspirational side of the nature of human beings. The spiritual side. It is not about religion. Rather, it is about our sense of purpose and meaning in life. The sense of making a contribution, of being the best that we can be. The idea of being part of, and contributing to, something bigger than us as an individual. This need to have a sense of contribution, purpose and meaning has been identified by psychologists as a fundamental need of human beings. In psychology it is often closely linked to the concepts of self-expression or self-actualization.

As I continued developing my Full Spectrum Life, my need to make a contribution to the planet became overwhelming. I could no longer ignore that voice in my head saying, "What difference are you making on the planet even though you are working so hard and giving so much time and energy to your work?"

Someone I used to know had a great phrase for this question. He used to say, *"What have you done for the planet today? Or are you just sucking air?"* I felt like I was just sucking air and yet depleting myself totally in the process.

Having moved away from that corporate role and added other businesses to my activities, I now feel like I am in fact making a difference in people's daily lives through the work that I do. If I can find a way to feel connected to a purpose and feel like I am making a difference, so can you!

My contribution pillar was very weak and low when I started down the path towards a Full Spectrum Life. I have come a long way since then. After making changes over a period of years, I now know that what I do every day in my work makes a difference.

As I started to look at my life in terms of contribution and what changes I could make in order to get a sense of purpose and meaning, I did consider whether there was a different way for me to be outside of work that would allow me to achieve a sense of meaningfulness. For some people this approach may be effective. My challenge was that my work took so much of my time and energy that it was difficult to see how I could find a way to engage in activities that would strengthen my contribution pillar outside of working hours. Therefore, my conclusion was that I needed to adjust my work to be more purposeful and meaningful. Your route to more meaning may be through work or it may be outside of your work. Your circumstances will be unique to you. Get creative and find what is effective for you.

Let's return to the Ancient Greeks again and their different words for love. The third word that I want to bring to mind is agape. This represents unconditional love. Love that just is. No strings attached. No reciprocation necessary. Just love.

Why have I brought agape love into the contribution pillar, the pillar about our spiritual nature, rather than the relationship pillar? The language I have used to describe agape love tells it all. Using the words "love that just is" puts it squarely in the spiritual realm. Agape love is omniscient and energy sourced. If you think about it, in the realm of spirit and the contribution pillar everything "just is". There is no right/wrong, male/female, positive/negative, us/them.

Have you ever experienced unconditional love? It is a blissful experience when it happens, however fleeting the moment of pure agape love may be. Everyone wants to be loved for who they are. In other words, everyone seeks agape love. Yet it can be difficult to give agape love. Many of the spiritual teachings are essentially driven by the goal of giving and receiving unconditional/agape love.

The power of focusing on contribution was very clear to me during my husband's illness and death, followed quickly by the same for my father. By focusing my attention on contribution to making their final life experience the best it could be, I found strength, acceptance, calmness and purpose.

Think back to the HIV-positive woman we met in Chapter 3. She rose above her grief, anger and despair by focusing on a purpose. She turned her tragic circumstances into the motivation to make a contribution. She used the credibility her experiences gave her, to raise awareness about HIV and about living as an HIV-positive person.

Recall too Doug's description of what became his purpose and passion: *"to guide, teach, lead and otherwise facilitate people on how to break through self-limiting beliefs and self-defeating behaviours. To create systems and methodologies that enables them to create a life of their choosing. To discover, or re-discover their purpose, their personal power, and their passion in life. To develop a truly meaningful life purpose. To be less driven by destructive emotions and negative paradigms, and to be more resourceful, more creative, more resilient and more determined to take charge of the quality of their own lives."*

Having dealt with the pure survival aspects of his early life, Doug went on to become the inspirational leader that he was through the development of, and then commitment to, this life purpose. His, in fact, had a double whammy; his purpose was to facilitate others achieving a life of purpose.

The contribution pillar is about the big questions:

- Who am I?
- Why am I here?
- What is my purpose?
- How can I make a difference?

To get answers to these questions we need to be still, be quiet and listen to our inner wisdom. Answers may take some time to emerge, not a popular notion in this day of instant everything. But perseverance and commitment to making time to be still and quiet will pay off.

This is another skill. It can be learned with guidance from an experienced teacher. If someone like me, always on the go, can learn to do this and now teach it, then so can you! We'll be exploring this later on in the book.

The Four Pillars Strength and Balance Assessment Tool

For a quick, yet highly insightful, look at the strength and balance of your Four Pillars, use this simple assessment tool.

1. On each axis mark where you perceive yourself to be in terms of the strength of your Four Pillars.
2. Be honest with yourself and remember the fullness of the definitions. For example, wealth is not just about money, but also about fun and learning.
3. Then join the four points to form a shape.

The dotted line diamond in the diagram below shows four strong pillars perfectly balanced. The more asymmetrical is your shape, then the more out of balance are your Four Pillars.

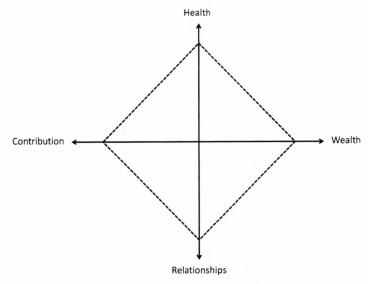

The Four Pillars Strength & Balance Chart

As an example, here is what my chart would have looked like if I had had this tool back in 1994 when I started down the path of personal development. It is small (not at its full potential) and it is asymmetrical (out of balance). It looks very different now.

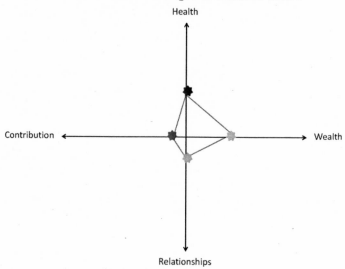

Four Pillars Strength & Balance Chart

Your chart may not be as asymmetrical as mine was. Perhaps your pillars are well balanced, but you want to take your life to the next level. To expand the size of your diamond. Whether it is asymmetry or the desire to expand your chart that brings you here, in either case the principles, concepts, tools and techniques set out in this book will help you to achieve a more symmetric and a larger diamond... a more balanced life and a higher level life. But... only if, you apply them!

Chapter 5: The Five Steps Growth Model

Are you beginning to see that to live life happily, effectively, productively, professionally and meaningfully we need to be on a path of personal growth? It is through personal growth that we strengthen and balance our four pillars and thus live life at a higher level.

The Five Steps Growth Model shows us the process of personal growth. It provides a framework through which we can observe ourselves in different stages of growth and guides us on to the next stage so that we can continue to grow and not get stuck.

Five Steps to Growth

Step 1: Confusion

Now some might say, "Oh boy, I've been on step one most of my life!" If we are human, if we are alive, is there going to be some confusion in our lives? Is it natural to have some confusion in our lives? For sure it is. As Jim Quinn used to say,

"People who don't have any confusion in their lives are in today's obituaries."

The biggest challenge about confusion is that it is so easy to get stuck there. To allow the confusion to freeze us, to stop all forward movement in our life. We need to welcome confusion, it is the first sign that we are about to grow! Another famous Jim Quinn saying,

"Hot dog I got some confusion!!"

I know how corny this phrase sounds, particularly to people outside North America. Believe me, it also sounds corny to Americans and Canadians! The corniness is actually part of how and why this little phrase works so well. Use it. Say it, either out loud or in your head, but with great enthusiasm whichever way you do it. This little phrase is a powerful tool. It will help you to avoid getting bogged down, discouraged and paralysed by confusion.

Step 2: Exploration

Remember the way I suggested to get the most out of this book? To pause and look deeper. In other words to explore. When confusion comes along, the second thing we are going to do (after saying to ourselves, "Hot dog I got some confusion") is to start to explore. To ask questions. To get curious and to look deeper at what is going on in our life. Where am I at? What is this about? What do I need to learn here? What has triggered this? What is going on under the surface?

Now it is not necessarily about getting clear, detailed answers to all these questions. The act of asking the questions in and of itself will shift awareness and create insights at levels that are not necessarily at the mental/analytical level. In fact, when we truly do dig deeper, the answers have little to do with the thinking part of us, rather they come to the intuitive part of us.

The danger with the exploration stage is that instead of becoming an explorer, we become an archeologist. We dig and we dig. Then we get more confused, so we dig some more. This often happens when we get stuck in the thinking part of ourselves and are not reaching the intuitive. We are stuck in the head rather than the mind.

To avoid this we need to move to step three.

Step 3: Incubation
We break through from the potential rabbit hole that is the confusion and exploration cycle with incubation.

Incubation is perhaps the most counter-cultural part of the five steps in society today. In today's world we want everything instantly, and for the most part we are used to getting everything immediately. We borrow rather than save up, we have instant access to more information than was imaginable even two decades ago right at our finger tips wherever we are. No need to wait for the shops to open to find something we want, just go on-line and order it there and then. We eat instant but nutrition-starved food. We expect immediate responses to phone calls, emails or texts, day or night. Life moves quickly. It seems like the pace of life is speeding up year by year. We try to do more. We are bombarded by data and, all the time, we are making choices in this mass of, often unintelligible, data.

Despite, or perhaps even because of, the speed of life today and the incessant bombardment with data, it is more important than ever to incubate. We need to be still, be quiet and go inside to be at peace and listen. This is where the ideas, alternatives, options, possibilities lie. This is where we can tap into the genius that resides in all of us. We can slow down the brain waves out of the analytical thinking mode and into the intuitive genius mode. Incubation is where we will find our options, possibilities, solutions and potentials. As a result, step 3, incubation, is where we empower ourselves.

In Chapter 9: The Power of the Mind you will learn more about how to incubate. In particular, we will explore a technique called centering which enables us to access the intuitive genius at will, rather than by chance.

Step 4: Illumination

As we patiently incubate, the moment of illumination will come. People describe illumination in different ways. Some call it an "ah-ha" moment. Others talk of the moment the light comes on. It's the eureka moment when we see a solution, the way forward, the possibilities that are in front of us. At this point we have moved to step 4 of the five steps to growth. Is that an energising moment?

Why do you think we hear so often of people who wake in the night with a great idea or having solved a problem that was troubling them? Because they stopped, they became still and quiet and allowed their wisdom to emerge from within.

The other place you hear of people getting their bright ideas is in the shower. Again, for a few moments they have stopped and detached from the mental hamster wheel and are sheltered from the data bombardment.

My illumination moments often occur while I am out on my daily walks with my dog. I get out into nature, detach from the computer, phones, emails and texts and slow my mind down. I give myself the opportunity to incubate and achieve illumination. And more often than not there is a solution, an idea, a new perspective.

Step 5: Celebration

Do you take life too seriously? Many of us do. We have to remember the fifth step is to celebrate. There was great song back in the late 1970's on the Kids from Fame album called Life is a Celebration. The music uplifts and empowers just like the moments of step 5 celebration do.

Take a moment to breathe, acknowledge and celebrate. This is the step that I most often miss out. I am too busy moving on to the next task.

But, can we get stuck in celebration? Just like all the other steps, we only spend as much time as we need to be ready to move on to the next.

And after celebration we will find ourselves at some point back at step 1. Hot dog I got some confusion! This time we are moving on to an even higher level. Each cycle takes us higher on our path of continuous improvement.

Look back at your life and you will see the pattern of The Five Steps Growth Model.

Now that you are aware of this process you can harness it. Feeling confused, then "Hot dog I got some confusion!" Time to do some exploration. Ok so I've been exploring this for a while now, maybe I should incubate. Take charge, make the choice to incubate. Then be alert to the ideas, solutions and possibilities that will emerge as you enter the illumination step. Enjoy a celebration of your life and then move onwards and upwards.

By consciously engaging this growth model, you will be more effective at creating your life on your terms, rather than life creating you.

Time for some exploration, incubation and possibly illumination now. Write some notes in your journal about where in the Five Steps Growth Model you have been living. Are you stuck in Step 1 and Step 2? Do you treat your life as a party and get stuck in Step 5? Do you incubate problems and situations or continue dashing headlong into everything? Are you listening closely enough to hear your wisdom giving you solutions and possibilities? Where have you been living and where do you want to be?

I'll wrap up this chapter with another phrase from Jim Quinn on personal growth:

"People are like fruit. When I'm green I grow,
when I'm ripe I rot!"

Or in the words of Jim Clemmer, a Canadian leadership author and corporate trainer:

"There's nothing more dangerous than a
comfortable rut."

Chapter 6: Where is Your "I AM" Hiding?

Authenticity, living the life we were meant to live, being true to ourselves, living life in alignment with who we really are, living life according to our own expectations not someone else's. These are all phrases we hear more often today as people start to recognise that the old formulae for success and supposed happiness don't work for everyone. We are all unique and, therefore, we all have unique ways of expressing ourselves through the life we choose to live.

Are you in the career or marriage you want or the one your parents wanted you to have? How many decisions have you made based on what other people might think rather than what your heart wanted? Did you get into the rat race quite willingly, but now recognize it is not for you? What creative gifts do you have that have been ignored for more career-oriented skills? Do you love to sing, to play music, to dance, to draw, to cook, to sew, to write, to take photographs, to do carpentry, to design clothes, to decorate? The possibilities for having a creative outlet are endless.

The Oxford English Dictionary defines self-actualisation as *"the realisation or fulfilment of one's talents and potentialities, especially considered as a drive or need present in everyone."* Set aside the generally accepted formulae for success and happiness, self-actualisation is key. Self-actualisation first came to the fore in the late 1930's and early 1940's. Maslow's Hierarchy of Needs, with self-actualisation at the top of the hierarchy, is perhaps the most famous application of the concept in that early period. It is useful to those of us wishing to live life at a higher level because it gives us a common concept to apply, whilst allowing absolutely unique expression of who I am within that framework.

When we are living life at a higher level we are becoming more and more who we **really** are. We are manifesting on the outside, more of the substance and values we have on the inside. Who we really are, and who the world sees, are in greater alignment. We are living in increasing integrity and authenticity, fulfilling more and more of our potentiality.

Why does that matter? Why is it important that we are able to live life as who we really are? What does it matter if we don't allow our creativity to surface? Why can't we just continue on with the misalignment between what we do and show on the outside and who we really are on the inside? Well, because when there is misalignment, there is tension, tightness, distress, dissatisfaction and, ultimately, dis-ease.

If it is so fundamental to human beings, why is this such a big deal? Why does it take such effort to find and then express who I really am? Where is my I AM hiding? And why is it hiding?

Natural Behaviour and Normal Behaviour

Pull out your journal, divide a page vertically down the middle and write "Natural" at the top of one half of the page. Think about a four year old child. Make a list of words under the heading Natural to describe a four year old child. Are they joyful, spontaneous, curious, honest? Do they express love or not? Do they have high self-esteem or low self-esteem? Do they trust? You get the idea… make a list under the heading Natural.

Now at the top of the second half of the page write the word "Normal". This time, think of the general adult population and write down words to describe them. Are they angry, tired, fearful, indifferent, depressed, low energy, closed? Do they have high self-esteem or low self-esteem? Do they trust?

Here's an example of the lists I came up with when I did this exercise.

NATURAL	NORMAL
Joyful	Depressed
Loving	Angry
Curious	Apathetic
Energetic	Addicted
Compassionate	Insecure
Spontaneous	Hurried
Sensitive	Self-righteous
Creative	Fearful
Peaceful	Reactive
Relaxed	Resentful
Expressive	Tired
Forgiving	Anxious
Trusting	Guarded

Look at these two lists. The Normal list are learned behaviours. They are what we pick up through life. The Natural list are not learned. They are the true essence of who I really am, of who you really are.

No wonder life gets a little challenging when we have to deal with all these Normal people surrounding us day in and day out!

In some way, at some time, these Normal behaviours that we learned have served us. However, the chances are that we have taken them on board to such an extent now, that they have become our habitual behaviours, rather than something that was only applicable in a specific circumstance at a specific time, now long gone.

Natural is who I am. Normal is what I have become. How do you want to live? Do you want to be Normal or Natural? Look again at the lists. Are you feeling ridiculous yet? We could be living in a world of all those Natural experiences. Instead we spend so much time being Normal. Which list is more mature? Which is more professional? Which is more attractive? Which is living life at a higher level?

This is why living an authentic life in alignment with who I really am is so important. Just look at the difference in our experience of the world if we are Natural rather than Normal! How can we possibly fulfill our potential and live life at a higher level when we are living as a Normal person? It is time to shift our consciousness to being Natural again.

Walls
Where have these Normal patterns come from? Think back to yourself as a child. Back to the time when you were free, enthusiastic, joyful and fearless. Even children like Doug, whose life turned traumatic at such an early age, have some experience of those Natural times.

At our core is the essence of who we really are, the I AM. That is where the Natural resides, where our genius and creativity is located. As a young child, the I AM is all pervasive. What is inside, is outside too. What happened?

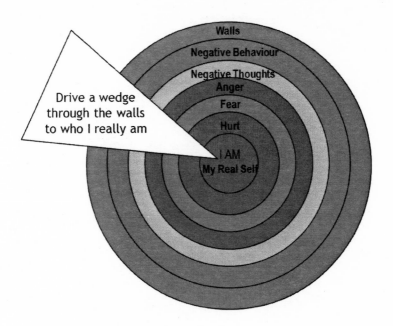

The central circle represents "I AM". The true essence of me. That part of me that shone as a child. But what happens to that I AM?

We get hurt. The hurt starts in childhood and continues through life. For Doug the death of his first adoptive mother when he was three years old was the point at which the hurt really started to bite. Though later in life, he also became aware of the hurt that he suffered as a result of being given up for adoption at birth by his mother.

The hurts are often not such dramatic events as the death of a parent or physical and emotional abuse. Little things cause hurt and pain too. Feeling left out by family or friends. Being the odd one out. A sharp word from a parent or teacher. Being told you are not good enough. The hurts are the first layer of covering that starts to hide our I AM.

I remember the start of my own hurts. The start of hiding who I really am, losing my enthusiasm and trying to be inconspicuous. I was six years old. We had moved to a small village in the Yorkshire Dales from Wakefield, a city in the industrial heartland of Yorkshire. We were only going to be there for a few months until our new home was built in Selby. It was a small insular community in those days, wary, and even hostile, to strangers and especially city folk. There was a two room schoolhouse in the village. One room for the infants, one for the juniors and a partition that was pulled open in the mornings for the whole school to have assembly together. Even at that age I felt that I was an outsider. I don't think I realised that being a city girl in a village was the reason, but I knew I was an outsider.

I was a clever little girl, enthusiastic about learning and wanting to please my parents and teachers. One clever boy in particular didn't like the fact that I was usurping the old hierarchy. I was seated opposite him in the classroom with four other children all around a big desk. I remember this boy, he was called Mark, seeking me out shortly after I joined the school and pushing me over in the playground. It was winter time so I was wearing thick woolen tights. My knees were badly grazed and my tights had big holes in them. In the days that followed, Mark didn't push me over again; instead he spent the day kicking my grazed, scabbed knees under the desk. Each night when I got home my mother had to bathe the wooly tights off my knees where the grazes had been reopened by the kicking and then dried up again.

I couldn't do anything about the fact that I was an outsider, but I could make myself as inconspicuous as possible. I didn't want to stand out. Here was a major misalignment at an early age for me, the little girl trying not to be different yet whose favourite character in Winnie the Pooh was Tigger because "the wonderful thing about Tiggers is I'm the only one." I learned to be as inconspicuous as I could.

Why? Because just like all of us when we are hurt in whatever way, I was afraid of getting hurt again. My fear of standing out as a clever girl and attracting the wrath of Mark, and maybe others too, was enough to teach me to be as inconspicuous as possible.

Fear is the next layer that covers our I AM. Fear of being hurt again. The next chapter looks in greater depth at fear.

Fear then creates negative feelings and emotions and we build another layer between the essence of I AM and what we are presenting on the outside. Perhaps the most common negative emotion is anger. It shows up in many different forms but anger is at the root of many negative feelings. Sometimes it is turned outwards. Sometimes it is turned inwards. Often depression is an expression of anger turned inwards. Other negative emotions and feelings that we layer between us and the outside world include helplessness, despair, grief, insecurity, guilt, jealousy, hatred, vengefulness, discouragement, worry, disappointment, overwhelm, frustration, pessimism and boredom.

There is a quote from Buddha that resonates very deeply with me, perhaps it will with you too:

*"You will not be punished **for** your anger, you will be punished **by** your anger."*

From the negative emotions comes negative thinking. Examples include angry thoughts, prejudice, destructive thought patterns, lack of clarity, obsessiveness, anxiety, self-righteous, suspicious, cynical, unforgiving. The list goes on! And we now have four layers between our I AM and the outside world.

All kinds of negative behaviours follow the negative thought patterns. Things like violence, self-harming, addiction, abusiveness, manipulation, controlling, shy, reactive, guarded, suppression, holding a grudge, discriminatory, vindictive, mean.

And finally around all of that we build walls to fend off the potential for pain. We become hard, brittle and prickly, rather than soft, flexible and strong. In trying to protect the essence of who I AM, I have cut off all access to that shining central core, the golden ball in Robert Bly's Iron John.

We learn to believe that these outer layers and the fortress wall is who I AM. Then we take that belief, that mental image and all the Normal emotions, thoughts and behaviours into our work and our personal relationships. Everywhere we look, our sense of needing to protect ourselves from hurt is reinforced: television, radio, print and web.

We are up against strong forces trying to keep us separated from the truth of who we really are. It will take commitment, integrity and courage to break through these walls. Is it worth driving that wedge through to allow who I really am to re-emerge? Absolutely it is. Only as we allow the inner essence of who we really are to get bigger, peeling away the layers we have built up through life can we begin to live with more integrity, authenticity and Naturalness. The tensions and dis-ease of being out of alignment with who we really are can begin to be relieved.

As with the other concepts of living life at a higher level through strengthening and balancing the four pillars of a Full Spectrum Life, the process of breaking through to the truth of who I AM and then allowing the light of that essence to wash away the layers of walls so that it shines as brightly to the outside world as it does inside its protective shield, is a life-long process.

Just because we are doing some personal development work doesn't mean that life won't keep throwing curve balls. Yes, there will still be hurts and pain. But as we peel away the layers and shine the light of who we really are, the walls we build with new hurts are much easier to break through than the first time we try to deal with an accumulation of a lifetime of wall building.

We also see the hurt and our response to it with a new perspective. That, in and of itself, makes the process of continuing to allow the I AM to shine in the world that much easier.

Chapter 7: Fear

Fear is a big subject. Of course there are things like fear of heights, fear of spiders, fear of snakes and fear of closed spaces. Yes, in some ways these can limit our lives. But the really big limitations come in the form of the fears that are about how we relate to people and to ourselves. You have seen in the previous chapter that fear is at the root of all negative feelings, thoughts and behaviours. This realization alone can dramatically change how we interact with the world.

First, there is what fear brings out in us. Take a moment to capture in your journal the kinds of negative emotions, thoughts and behaviours fear typically triggers in you. How does that impact your interactions with the world and your self- image? Is your fear rational? Are you truly in danger? Think about and write down where you learned these fear reactions. Did you get laughed at for being compassionate and then learned to be tough? Did you comply when you were put down for being creative? Did you choose shyness as a result of getting yelled at? Did you get angry for being belittled?

Secondly, when we recognize that fear underlies negativity going on around us, or directed at us, it changes how we see the person. It increases the probability that we will deal with the person in a compassionate, empowering and proactive manner rather than being sucked into negative behaviour ourselves.

Let me ask you to think about this. If you had to relate to you, to deal with your reactions, would you be able to do it?

Imagine what it must be like to try to deal with you when you are reacting from fear. Would you react back to you?

The next time someone starts reacting angrily, you can have the vision to look past their outer reaction and look for what they are protecting with their anger. Almost certainly it will be some form of sensitivity. What if they are behaving arrogantly towards you? Look beyond the arrogance and see that at some level they are protecting their insecurity. If they are shut down, look for the creativity they are protecting.

Doing personal development work around fear isn't about eliminating feeling fear. It is about recognizing when fear is about to take you down a path that doesn't serve you and, instead, choosing to take charge and make your own decision, rather than letting fear make your choice on what to do, or think, and how you behave.

Susan Jeffers' classic book, Feel the Fear and Do It Anyway: How to Turn Your Fear and Indecision into Confidence and Action, also recognizes that fear will always be there. She says,

"Fear will never go away as long as I continue to grow."

And she concludes that,

"Pushing through fear is less frightening than living with the underlying fear that comes from a feeling of helplessness."

Let's go back to the "I AM" at the centre of our being. The essence of who we truly are. Here reside our gifts, our

Naturalness, our light and our vision. Fear of being hurt in some way gradually starts to cut us off from the I AM. How does that happen?

It starts out with the way we react to a circumstance. Perhaps as a child we drew a red ocean instead of a blue ocean and were chastised for colouring it wrongly. Different people will react in different ways to that circumstance. Some will get angry, some will become shy and withdrawn, some will suppress their creativity and some will turn their anger inwards.

What about a child whose compassion allows them to see both sides of an argument. When they see two friends fighting they try to stop the fight using their compassion. Getting in the middle of a fight results in them getting hurt. What has this child learned? "If I express my compassion I get hurt. Instead I'll become judgmental and take one side or another." That way the child makes one friend and achieves some acceptance. But they hide their gift behind the wall of fear resulting from hurt.

Doug was different from the rest of the family he was adopted into. He thought differently, his emotional nature was different, his values were different. Even as a boy this was evident. His father tried to beat him into fitting in. But how could that work? You can't beat the essence of someone out of them; you can only beat them into covering up that essence with negative feelings, thoughts and behaviours. Somehow, even at just 15 years old, Doug knew that for him to survive he had to leave that family.

As a child we are playing and experimenting with our creativity, or our spontaneity, or our kindness, or our passion. Sometimes we get taken advantage of or become the target for anger and we react. We protect that gentleness, or that vision, or that creativity with hardness, or insecurity, or quietness, or shyness, or arrogance, or sarcasm, or whatever it is for you.

Many people say, "But I don't know what these gifts at the core of my I AM are. How can I let them shine if I don't know what they are? How can I be who I truly am if I don't know what that is?" I remember doing an experiential exercise in a personal development programme which required me to look back on my childhood, to visualize myself as a child and to experience how I was as a child. This was meant to give me some insight into my gifts, the things that I have protected through my fear reactions. But I was a total blank. I seemed to have no memory of myself as a child. Certainly no memory of how I felt as a child. Perhaps the answer is there... I felt nothing, I felt numb, I had cut myself off for some reason. What had I shut down? Spontaneity? Playfulness? Exuberance? All the things I had been "shushed" for when my dad was working nights.

We can use our fear reactions to get a glimpse into our I AM essence and the gifts it contains. Since our fear reactions are there to protect some part of our I AM, when we find ourselves on the threshold of a fear reaction, we have the opportunity to look beyond the fear and see what it is we are protecting. When we discover what we have been protecting, then we uncover the tools we need to get whatever it is we long for in our life.

If we find ourself getting into trouble every time we, metaphorically, colour outside the lines, then soon instead of just reacting to the circumstance we start to "pre-act". We start to take on anger, arrogance, shyness, or whatever, before the circumstance even arises! This soon becomes a habit and eventually it becomes our self-image.

Instead of having feelings we become them. I feel angry turns into I AM angry. I feel stupid turns into I AM stupid. I feel unworthy turns into I AM unworthy. I feel shy turns into I AM shy. I feel insecure turns into I AM insecure.

Many people spend their lives focused on trying to conjure up a perfect set of circumstances that will never trigger their anger, arrogance, shyness, insecurity, unworthiness... It is pretty much a futile exercise. Only by breaking through the walls created by fear and allowing the essence of who we truly are to shine through can we begin to find happiness. Happiness and peace comes not from perfect circumstances, but from inside the core of who we truly are, the I AM.

How do we do that? Little by little we change our habits. Instead of pre-acting with our Normal behaviours, we choose to share our I AM with the world. Have you ever asked yourself, "How come sometimes I can hit major problems and handle them like a superstar, and other times I get completely thrown off balance?" If comes down to whether you are responding from your I AM toolbox of gifts or from your fears.

At the moment you would normally justify protecting your I AM with hardness, or anger, or insecurity, or shyness, or shutting down, instead you can allow your I AM – creativity, love, passion - to shine. Of course this needs to be done with maturity, balance, consciousness and care. As an adult we can notice the fear, watch for pitfalls and danger zones, but continue sharing our I AM in a considered manner.

Is the Danger Real or Perceived?

There is a big difference between real danger of being harmed and the perceived danger that causes most of the fear that holds us back in life. Fear can serve a useful purpose when it makes us respond to a real danger in such a way as to keep us safe.

However, the fear we need to overcome as we start to work on personal development is the fear that is in response to a perceived, rather than a real, danger. For example, shutting down as a result of the fear of getting beaten for expressing our selves may have kept us safe as a small child, but it doesn't help us to get a job, have fulfilling relationships and be who we really are as an adult. The danger of being beaten has passed. But the behavior in the form of shutting down has become a programme, part of our self-image, which no longer serves.

I experienced firsthand the difference between real and perceived danger and the overwhelming fear that a perceived risk can generate. I was participating in an outward bound-type leadership programme. One of the exercises involved climbing up a telegraph pole, standing on a little platform on the top, then jumping off. I was in a harness with several ropes attached to me. On the end of each rope were three or four people ready to take the strain if I fell and when I jumped. Rationally, there was negligible risk that I would be hurt in any way. I saw several people do the exercise with no problems and no difficulty on the part of those taking the strain on the safety ropes. Yet I was terrified. I sat on the ground at the bottom of the pole in floods of tears for about 45 minutes. I was so afraid. Why? It was totally irrational and I knew it. Yet I was overwhelmed by fear. In the end, I am happy to say, that I overcame that fear and I did climb the pole and jump off. It illustrated very clearly to me how perceived risk can paralyse me if I let it.

The other lesson that was so clearly illustrated in this situation is that, when I allow fear to stop me in my tracks, I am not in a position to give of myself, to share my gifts, to lend support to others. All the time I was in tears at the bottom of the telephone pole, I was not helping everyone else by being on the end of a support rope.

I have also experienced the complete opposite… a fire walk. Rationally, there is no way that I should have been able to walk over those red hot coals without getting burned. Was I afraid? Yes I was, until I decided that I would do it. That took a long time, I was almost the last to go out of about 100 people on my stretch of hot coals! By the way, they kept replenishing the coals from the main fire so that they didn't cool down. Having made the decision, I knew that to keep myself safe I had to stay "in state" as Anthony Robbins, who was leading the process, called it. That meant abolishing fear from my mind. Yeah I did it! If I can walk on fire I can do pretty much anything I put my mind to!

Fear and Longing
Albert Einstein was not just a brilliant scientist. He also studied the human condition. He put forward the idea that there are two drivers of human behavior: fear and longing. This theme was taken up by many others since he wrote the article in 1930. Anthony Robbins expounds clearly on this notion in his audio programme, Get the Edge. We make our choices driven either by a desire to move away from something or avoid something,

or by a desire to move towards something, to get more of something. In other words we are driven by fear or by longing.

In fact, as we move through life making our choices, both fear and longing are usually in operation at the same time. The question is, does the fear win or does the longing win. For example, when you feel rejection, you are also battling a longing for love or acceptance. If the longing for love overcomes the fear, you ask for the date. But if the fear overcomes the longing, you don't. Each time your choice comes from fear you reinforce and strengthen that fear. Each time you move towards what you want, that becomes stronger.

Mother Theresa went into some parts of the world that are very dangerous. She went there with caution. She was a highly aware woman. She knew where danger was. But the danger was not enough to stop her from giving. The moral of the story: find a way to give, carefully.

Reactions to Fear

You are probably aware of the classic model of reaction to fear known as fight or flight. The model says that, when faced with fear, people will either fight or they will run away.

In his People Wheel and more recently in his book, The Love-based Leader, James Rosswell Quinn expanded on this classic model to give a more comprehensive view of reactions to fear. He suggests that there are, in fact, four reactions to fear that people exhibit. They can manifest in different ways, but essentially they fall into one of four categories:

- Fight;
- Flight;

- Freeze; or
- Façade.

Typically, we tend to lean towards one or other of these fear reactions. However, that doesn't mean that we only respond in one way. Different circumstances and internal states will bring out different fear reactions in the same person.

The fight and flight reactions are well documented. We get angry or we run away and avoid. Flight can also involve withdrawing inwardly, without actually physically running away. What about freeze? What does that look like? When I was sitting paralysed at the bottom of the telephone pole unable to say, "I'm next," I was in freeze. When we shut down our creativity, spontaneity, passion, expressiveness. That is also freeze. Façade means that we wear a mask for the outside world, pretending that everything is OK whilst on the inside we are in turmoil.

Understanding these four fear reactions helps with understanding ourselves, gives us the ability to choose to counteract these reactions, helps us to understand others and communicate and relate with people more skilfully, compassionately and effectively.

The Opposing Forces to Fear Reactions
Each of the four fear reactions has an opposing force that moves you from fear-based reaction to proactive response, if you apply it. The key is to be aware of what is going on for you. To be conscious of how you are about to react, or are reacting. As soon as you notice a fear reaction, then choose to oppose it, rather than allowing the reaction to take over and make your choices on thoughts, feelings and behaviours for you. This takes practice.

It takes awareness. It takes monitoring of your thoughts, feelings and behaviours. It requires you to live mindfully rather than unconsciously. But it can transform your life.

With practice, you will find that, rather than first reacting from fear and then choosing to oppose that reaction, you are able to choose the opposing force before the fear reaction has manifested. As Stephen Covey says, we are "response-able", if we take notice and make our choice from our centre, our I AM, instead of from fear. Finally your I AM can start to emerge again from behind the walls built up over years of fear-based reactionism.

So what are the opposing forces to the four fear reactions?:

- Fight is opposed by Courtesy. Instead of reacting angrily, choose courtesy and politeness.
- Flight is opposed by Integrity. Instead of running away, literally or figuratively, stand your ground.
- Freeze is opposed by Openness. Instead of shutting down, be open, reach into your I AM and express it.
- Façade is opposed by Ethics. Instead of pretending and wearing a mask, admit to yourself and others what is going on for you.

Focusing on living life from the point of view of courtesy, integrity, openness and ethics rather than from fight, flight, freeze and façade, can transform your life for the better and the ripple effect on those around you will astound you.

A word of caution though. As with the four pillars of a Full Spectrum Life, these four fear-opposing forces need to be balanced. As we focus on making choices that manifest courtesy, integrity, openness and ethics, we will be strengthening them all. However, they need to be applied with balance, otherwise we end up back in the fear reactions. For example, fight is really ethics without courtesy. Façade is courtesy without ethics.

The four fear reactions and their opposing forces is a powerful concept, the implications of which will unfold over many years as you put the concept into practice and become more and more skillful.

Fear of Rejection

Perhaps the most common fear is the fear of rejection. It comes in many guises. Rejection may take the form of violence, withdrawal, abandonment, belittlement, ignoring someone, trying to change someone, not accepting someone for who they are, making them wrong, stamping on creativity, spontaneity or passion, judging and shutting down communication, to name but a few.

Equally, reactions to the fear of rejection manifest in many ways. Some react with shyness, others react by becoming abusive, some are isolated or tough. Perhaps as a child you reacted with shyness, but now you have become tough. You may have changed your reaction, but you are still protecting and hiding your I AM.

For most people, even those in highly abusive relationships, the actual rejection really only takes place a small fraction of the time. However, the fear of rejection can be present and influencing our choices, most of the time. Therefore, it is how we deal with this fear of rejection that can make a big impact on our life experience.

Fear of rejection will likely always be there to some degree or another, no matter how much personal development work we do. What changes is how we deal with that fear. What choices we make when faced with that fear. To paraphrase William Penn Patrick,

"To be afraid is to be alive. To act despite that
fear is to be a leader."

How much of your life has the fear of rejection directly affected your choices, your vision, your peace, your attitude, your life? Not actually being rejected, but the fear of being rejected. The fear of what they will think, of what they might do, what I might get, or what I might look like, or what they might not do, of what I might lose, how it might appear, or what they will think about me? Be honest with yourself. I can say for myself, and for Doug up to the end of his life, that even with all the work we have done over the years, fear of potential rejection still impacts choices. To a lesser degree as time goes on, but still it is there.

Why do we fear rejection so much? Because when it does happen, when we are rejected, it hurts a lot. We feel stupid, unwanted, unimportant, unnecessary, betrayed, scorned, belittled, abused, abandoned or pitied. We feel let down when promises are broken, even if there is always a good excuse. What about when the people that were supposed to protect you were the ones hurting you? The ones that should have been committed to you were the ones that lied to you? The ones that were supposed to want to be with you were too busy? And what about putting the shoe on the other foot? How many times have you reacted to the fear of rejection and contributed to someone else experiencing these feelings?

When the fear of rejection is making my choices for me I don't put myself into the environment that I fear may result in rejection. By fearing rejection I don't go, I take myself out of the game and I miss out on an experience.

Let me give you an example from my life. Doug and I used to ballroom and Latin dance together. I love it. Since Doug died, of course I don't have a partner to dance with. Thanks to our superb, kind teacher and the generously supportive group of people we danced with in Kelowna, I felt able to continue to go to those classes on my own. Then I moved to the UK. This was a whole new ball game. What would people think of me showing up to ballroom dance classes on my own? Would I cope being the odd one out all the time? Would I be shunned? Would they think I'm weird? Thankfully my longing to dance overcame my fear of rejection and I started going to classes. It took courage to walk into the room the first time... actually it still does today. But I am so glad that I do every week. I would be missing out on such a great experience, and some lovely people, if I hid at home afraid of being rejected.

Fear of rejection means that we may push away something that might have been valuable. We don't say hello to someone and miss out on a great conversation or even relationship. May be we lash out at someone and in the process create guilt and shame in our self.

We don't like the feeling that comes with the fear of rejection. And, while the fear is making our choices for us, we will attack, run away, shut down or lie to avoid it. This is why people react to you and why you react to them. The antidote, the way to take control, is to oppose the fear reaction with courtesy, integrity, openness and ethics.

So write some more in your journal. What have you needed to do, that a fear has kept you from? Who have you needed to touch, that a little resentment has kept you from reaching? What have you needed to forgive that some doubts have kept you clinging onto? What have you needed to create and didn't yet? Who have you needed to inspire and not taken the opportunity?

Our Deepest Fear

I would like to close this chapter with the famous quotation from Marianne Williamson's book A Return to Love. It is poignant and at the same time cuts to the chase like a knife. Read it, reflect and look deeper.

> *"Our deepest fear is not that we are inadequate. Our deepest fear is that we are powerful beyond measure. It is our light, not our darkness that most frightens us. We ask ourselves, "Who am I to be brilliant, gorgeous, talented, fabulous? Actually, who are you NOT to be? … Your playing small does not serve the world. There is nothing enlightened about shrinking so that other people won't feel insecure around you. We are all meant to shine, as children do. We were born to make manifest the glory that is within us. It's not just in some of us; it's in everyone.*

And as we let our own light shine, we unconsciously give other people permission to do the same. As we are liberated from our own fear, our presence automatically liberates others."

Chapter 8: Trust

Fear and lack of trust go hand in hand. The fact that you are afraid of being rejected by someone means that you do not trust them to accept you. For example, if you are afraid that your friend will judge you if you do something you want to do, then you do not trust that friend to love and accept you.

When you are afraid of whether you can successfully do something, your self-talk is asking you what makes you think you can do that, then in fact you do not trust yourself to succeed. For example, someone who has found it difficult to be faithful in relationships in the past might not trust themselves to remain faithful in their current relationship. In doing so, they will most likely sabotage the relationship in some way.

Over the years, in workshops, I have seen the same response to a simple question. "How many here think they are trustworthy?" 99% of people in the room raise their hands. And similar results for the follow up question. "How many here want to be loved or trusted unconditionally?" Again 99% of the hands are raised.

We all think we are trustworthy, but do we trust ourselves? We all want to be trusted and loved unconditionally, but do we love and trust others unconditionally?

There's a story Doug used to tell to illustrate what is going on here. He used to say that there once was a man living in a cabin in the woods. In the cabin he had a beautiful wood stove. The stove could provide him with heat through the long winters and a means of cooking. The man used to stand in front of wood stove and say, "When you give me heat, I'll give you wood."

Just as we gain great insight into our gifts, and the true essence of the I AM at our core, by looking at what our fear reactions – fight, flight, freeze and façade - have been protecting, so too can looking at our patterns of trusting and not trusting.

Time to pause and look deeper. What are your patterns of not trusting? Have you been hurt by someone and had it affect who you trust now? Who do you trust? Who don't you trust? Are there patterns to who you trust and who you don't trust? Young? Old? Male? Female? Suits? Workers? Men with beards? Women with tattoos? A certain accent? The list goes on... It is worth taking a bit of time to look deeply at your own patterns of trust, especially in relationships that are difficult or fragile.

When we meet people, we form judgments about them so quickly. The most fundamental judgment we make in those first 30 to 60 seconds (I am being generous here) is whether or not we trust them.

You will never know how many remarkable relationships you have missed out on, whether they might have been just a few moments of conversation or lifelong friendships, because of not trusting someone, including yourself. You didn't trust them so you didn't have a conversation with them. You didn't trust them so you dumped them before they dumped you. You didn't trust yourself so you didn't go for that job.

The insane part of our trust patterns is that, for the most part, they are based on historical experiences, or hearsay, not on our actual experience of that person. Until we learn to trust and love unconditionally, letting go of the past, we bring our past experiences into our current relationships.

Over the next few days as you go about your daily activities, start to become conscious of what is going on with you around trust. Start to observe yourself as you interact with people. Notice what your trust reaction is when you come across someone in the street. There are three different ways we typically respond around trust. We say to ourselves:

- I trust you;
- I don't trust you; or
- I don't know if I trust you or not.

Start to be conscious about which of these three responses you engage when you meet someone or see people. Look for patterns. Do you have a default setting of trusting or not trusting? Do you trust certain types of people and not trust other groups of people? Do you find it difficult to trust one sex or the other? Do you find it difficult to trust younger people? Or older people?

Do you tell yourself you can't possibly know if you trust someone or not because you have only just met them and don't know them? Of course, what this really means is that you don't trust them. If you did, you would.

Our attitude of trusting, or not trusting, changes the effectiveness of our interactions with people. It changes our whole demeanor as we engage with people. If we are trusting of our self and others, we are much more likely to be open, honest, spontaneous, generous and kind for example. In short, the chances of us dealing with the person in a Natural way, in alignment with who we really are at the essence of our I AM, is much higher. As we interact with them in a Natural way, then we are also much more likely to see them as they truly are, to see their I AM shining through.

It is difficult to be fearful at the same time as trusting. Conversely when we don't trust we are also fearful. Since fear is the source of all negative thoughts, feelings and behaviours, then if we can avoid being fearful by trusting, then we can avoid negativity.

The Trust Formula
You might be reading this thinking, "Easier said than done." In this section I am going to show you a simple tool that Jim Quinn passed on to Doug. Use it to invoke a trusting response from yourself. This is something that can be applied at any moment, in any situation. It comes down to a simple formula. Doug used to say this formula is the secret to life. It is short, simple and life changing.

Formula A
I love you, and I accept you,
Even though I don't understand you.

Take a careful look at that. Say it to yourself. Say it out loud. How do you feel as you say it? Do you feel grounded, centered, trusting, loving, accepting, compassionate, strong, courageous?

Notice that Formula A does not say it is OK that the person is reacting however they are reacting. It just says that you love and accept them even though you have no idea why they are reacting so irrationally, angrily, crazily, selfishly… you fill in the blanks. In essence, Formula A separates the behavior from the person. I may not condone the behavior, but I can still love and accept the person.

Nor does it say that I have to put myself into a dangerous situation where I, or others, may be harmed. I love you and I accept you even though I don't understand why you are lashing out and I am going to move away from here as quickly as I can.

Do you think that little formula could improve any difficult or challenging relationships you have in your life? Perhaps with children, parents, boss, spouse, co-workers? I can tell you from my own experience, as well as feedback from others who have learned to use this tool, that it dramatically changes the quality of relationships.

Almost all the time, Formula A is an internal tool. It is something that you will say silently in your head. Perhaps there are certain people to whom you could effectively say it out loud. However, notice it is not about changing their state or their reaction, it changes how *you* feel and how *you* respond. Therefore, it really doesn't need to be spoken out loud. It is about you. The other person does not need to hear for it to be effective.

Some people have a tough time with the word "love" in some contexts. For example, people will say, "But I don't love my boss and never will." If this is a stumbling block for you, there is a small change to make to the formula so that you can get some benefit from this tool, rather than no benefit because you won't use it. For situations like work, you can replace the word "love" with the word "respect". So, only if you need to, you can use "I respect you and I accept you even though I don't understand you."

Now let's take a look at the flip side of Formula A.

Formula B
I don't understand you,
Therefore I don't love you,
I don't accept you,
I don't trust you,
And I build walls.

This would be the Normal formula for life. Take a good look. How often do you find yourself implementing Formula B in your relationships?

Say Formula B to yourself. Say it out loud. Is there a difference in how you feel, your energy, when you say Formula B versus Formula A? To me, Formula B feels tight, anxious, fearful, aggressive, i.e. Normal. So the question is how do you want to live your life? Do you want to live Normally or Naturally?

Many people are very hard on themselves. They are critical of themselves, unsure of themselves, they feel unworthy or undeserving, they don't trust their own abilities or judgment. I would go as far as to say that even the most evolved and enlightened person will from time to time have those thoughts and feelings. In essence, what we are doing when we get into that territory is we are applying Formula B to ourselves:

I don't understand myself,
Therefore I don't love myself,
I don't accept myself,
I don't trust myself,
And I build walls.

Focus on that for a few minutes. Look for examples in your life where you have applied Formula B to yourself and then recognize the consequences. Now is a good time to pause, look deeper and write some notes in your journal.

Say Formula B using myself out loud. How does that feel? I've seen all kinds of reactions to this. Some people laugh out loud because they feel so ridiculous when they realize what they have been doing to themselves and the impact that it has had on their lives. Others react with great sadness and a feeling of "what a waste".

The important thing here is to get the insights, but then let it go. Don't now continue to apply Formula B as you learn this lesson! Make a shift and start to apply Formula A to yourself.

Formula A for Myself
I love myself, and I accept myself,
Even though I don't always understand myself.

Do you think this might work better for you? Instead of being hard on yourself, using Formula B on yourself, make a conscious switch to using Formula A on yourself. Watch out for the times when you start heading down the Formula B route and, as fast as you can, make the switch to Formula A.

Contrast how you feel when you say Formula A about yourself and when you say Formula B. Which gives you energy? Which is positive and courageous? Which serves you?

Using Formula A as the basis for your interactions with others and with yourself, changes the quality of those interactions dramatically. Not only does it change how you respond in a situation, but that then has a ripple effect on the people you are dealing with. As you are calm, centered and responsive rather than reactive, the energy of the interaction changes and more often than not your centeredness rubs off on those around you.

Chapter 9: The Power of The Mind

The Power of the Mind is a vast subject. Science is slowly catching up with ancient wisdom that, for millennia, has placed an emphasis on using the mind. If you have an interest, and start digging, you will find so much teaching and research in this field. Some of my favourite writings on the subject are from Abraham-Hicks and from Buddhist teachers.

This chapter is about the practicalities of harnessing the power of your mind. I will not pretend to be offering a complete, in depth thesis on the subject of the mind. However, in this chapter you will gain an understanding of the impact of programming and habitual mind patterns, the structure of the mind and its different functions and learn a powerful tool for harnessing the power of your mind at will.

Dr Denis Waitley was one of the first people to use the power of the mind to enhance the performance of elite athletes. Do you think he was greeted with some skepticism at the time? Today I doubt that there is a single professional athlete who does not use mind tools, such as visualization, in their preparation, training and performance. Dr Waitley then went on to apply similar approaches with other high performance individuals such as company CEOs and NASA astronauts.

The power of the mind is not just about finding the way to super human performance in extreme endeavour though. It is about living moment by moment, day by day, in clarity, balance, harmony, centeredness, courage and decisiveness. You may have different words to describe this state, but I have never met anyone who did not aspire to it. So what gets in the way? People want to live in this state, whether they declare that consciously or not. We all have a mind; therefore we all have the power to live in this state. So why don't we? For some it is ignorance of the fact that they have a choice, lack of knowledge of the tools, or lack of self-discipline to apply the tools if they know them, and then there are our programmes.

Programming

What do I mean by programming? We have already discussed the distinction between reacting to a situation and responding to a situation. When we react, we go into automatic pilot basing our thoughts, feelings and behaviours on old situations and their consequences rather than the *present* situation and its consequences. After a while of reacting in a certain way, we start to pre-act. In other words, we start to think, feel and behave in those ways *before* the situation has even arisen. This way of being becomes a habit and eventually a programme where we start to define ourselves by that way of thinking, feeling or behaving. For example, I am angry, I am depressed, I am sickly, I am anxious, I am a victim, I always mess up relationships, and so on.

Henry Ford, founder of the Ford Motor Company, is credited with coining the phrase,

> *"If you always do what you have always done,*
> *you'll always get what you have always got."*

As human beings we are blessed with the opportunity to not "always do what we have always done." We have the choice to change our responses to fit the current situation and circumstances. In doing so, we have the opportunity to change our outcomes.

Programmes are often what sabotage our balance. Most programmes are initiated during early childhood. It has been said, that as adults we live our life on the programmes we learned as a child. Some say those programmes are in place by the time we are as young as three years old.

Think about that! Many of us are living a good portion of our adult lives based on what we had learned by the age of three or four years old! Does that not sound a little insane to you? I know that there have been times when I have felt that I am witnessing the behavior of a very large three year old in front of me. And no doubt there have been times when someone has thought the same about me! It is time to move beyond your programmes. You don't have to continue doing what you have always done.

We can distinguish two types of programmes: survival and non-survival programmes. For example, one survival program is "Look both ways before you cross the road". Have you learned that one so well that you look both ways even when you are on a one way street? Is that an important programme to keep you safe, both as a child and today?

It is the non-survival programmes that cause most of the problems. An example that starts out as protection for a child but then becomes a programme that does not serve an adult is, "Don't talk to strangers." It is a programme taught to a child to protect them. But then, what happens as an adult when you find yourself in a sales position having to do cold calling? Don't talk to strangers is now a non-survival programme that undermines your ability to function as you need to. The programme served a three year old, it no longer serves a 30 year old.

We learn our programmes from the people around us. The most obvious source is our parents, or those parenting us. However, the circle of people influencing our programmes is much wider than that. For example, siblings, extended family, friends of parents, playmates, social groups such as churches, teachers and, increasingly, media. Some examples of non-survival programmes include:

- Low self-esteem
- Anger
- Abuse of alcohol or drugs
- Negative attitude
- Won't or can't share love
- Smoking
- Shame
- Guilt
- Withdrawn
- Feeling unworthy or undeserving
- Poverty mentality
- Irresponsible money management
- Violence
- Victim mentality
- Undemonstrative
- Fearful

The list goes on. You can probably add to it from your own experience.

The first step in breaking free from your unproductive programmes is recognizing the ones that are still running your life for you. Please take a few minutes now to pause, look deeper and journal about your programmes that are not serving you as you live in your life today. Think about your childhood and the programmes you learned back then but which today take you out of balance with your Four Pillars.

Remember, this is the first step to breaking free. There is hope for us as human beings because we are the only creatures on earth that can change. As we break free from the programmes that are running our lives, move away from operating on auto pilot, then we can tap into the power of our mind to live in clarity and balance with courage, trust and love as the basis of our choices instead.

A Model of the Mind

The mind is more than the brain. Certainly it involves the brain, but it is more than the supercomputer between our ears. When I think of my mind, I sense it at my solar plexus with tentacle-like pathways throughout my body, including a connection to my brain.

My understanding of the mind is similar to the Buddhist concept of mind which brings together the wisdom of the head with the compassion of the heart.

Scientific knowledge and study of the brain is advancing rapidly. As the science of the brain is developing, it is leading to the scientific recognition of the additional dimension that the mind has, beyond the mechanics of the brain.

A simple and helpful model of the mind involves the recognition of two parts: the objective and the subjective, or the outer and the inner. The objective part is the outer physical body. The subjective is the inner spiritual part of ourselves.

The objective mind is the part of the mind that we begin to develop through schooling and through what our parents, and the others around us, teach and demonstrate to us. In the objective part of the mind we *think* we know. When we are operating from the outer mind, our brainwaves are measured in the range of 14-21 cycles per second. Brain technologists refer to this range as beta brainwaves.

The outer mind is analytical, using reason and logic to reflect information into our lives. It is where our programmes and Normal thoughts, feelings and behaviours come from (since much of the reason and logic we apply is flawed!)

This is the part of the mind where we pay tuition. On average, it costs tens, if not hundreds, of thousands to develop this part of someone's mind. And after all that time, resources and money in schooling, people's lives still don't work very well. Why? Because we have lost the connection to the other part of our mind, the subjective, inner part.

The subjective mind, the inner mind, is the part of the mind where we have intuition. It is where we sense what we know. It is the knowing part of the mind it is where we *know* we know rather than thinking we know.

Doug and Jim Quinn used to tell a funny little story to illustrate the difference between thinking you know and knowing you know.

There once was a husband and wife with nine children. They had just moved to a new town and it was the first day of school. Both parents went with the children to the new school. They all went to meet the Principal. There was a long bench outside the Principal's office where the children all sat in a row along the bench. Mother sat at one end and father at the other. The Principal came out and said to the father, "Are these your nine children?" He replied, "I think they are." Then the Principal went to the other end of the bench and said to the wife, "Are these your nine children?" She replied, "I know they are."

I truly believe that every single one of us has genius residing within. Our genius lies in the inner mind. Here we can access our creativity and inspiration. Our Natural self is expressed from the inner mind and our subconscious mind creates understanding.

Given that our genius, creativity, Naturalness and intuition are all part of the inner mind, it is surprising that, typically, we spend so little time, money and effort developing this part of our mind. Just as the outer mind can be developed so can the inner.

When we are operating from the inner mind, our brainwaves are slower than when we are operating from the outer mind. From the inner mind, they are measured at 7-13 cycles per second. This range is referred to as alpha brainwaves.

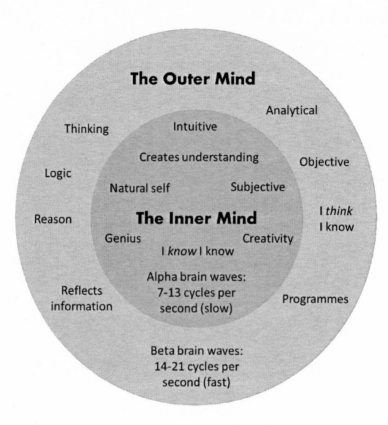

The outer and inner minds contain dualities, one element balancing the other. If we develop one mind and not the other, then automatically there are going to be imbalances in our life. For example:

- The objective part of the outer mind is where we live in the physical realm and needs to be balanced by the subjective part of the inner mind where we live in the spiritual realm.

- The creativity of the inner mind is balanced by the reason of the outer mind.
- Our programmes residing in the outer mind are balanced by our Natural self which resides in the inner mind.

The pairing of the outer mind as it reflects information and the inner mind as it creates understanding can be viewed in terms of the sun and the moon.

The inner mind is like the sun. It is the source of our power, light and energy. Another parallel is the golden ball in Robert Bly's Iron John. It is the centre of creative forces. Interesting how I sense my mind at my solar plexus, my sun centre.

The outer mind is like the moon. It reflects the light of the sun, the inner mind. What we manifest in the physical world through our outer mind is a reflection of what is shining at our sun centre. It is a reflection of the light of understanding and awareness created in our inner mind, our spiritual world.

What happens if we block off or shut down our connection to the sun at the centre of our being, our inner mind? We get disconnected from our inner mind through fear, anger, guilt and all the other Normal thoughts, feelings and behaviours. How can we reconnect and then stay connected so that we are operating from a balanced mind?

The key is in the brain science that has identified the difference in the speed of brainwaves when we are operating from the outer mind versus the inner mind.

Centering

There are a number of significant, scientific studies of meditators that measure brain waves and other brain activity. Whilst it has been recognized in the West for at least 50 years (much longer in the East) that our brainwaves slowdown from beta levels to alpha levels when we are in a centered and meditative state, recent studies are looking much deeper than that simple measure.

If the key to reconnecting and staying connected with our inner mind is to operate from alpha brainwave range, then, if we can learn how to instigate that state at will, we can access our inner mind at will.

Pause a moment here. Read that last sentence again. A simple little sentence you could so easily skip over. But take a moment to think about the implications of that sentence. Learn to slow down your brainwaves and gain access to your inner mind at will… your intuition, your genius, your creativity, your truth, your clarity, your solutions, your understanding, your light, your power, your energy.

Alexander Everett, known as the father of the human potential movement and the teacher of teachers, was a pioneer in the use of what he called "alpha thinking" in personal development. He introduced alpha thinking in the Mind Dynamics self-improvement seminar in 1968 and went on to teach the founders of many personal development programmes including Jim Quinn, who trained Doug, Werner Erhardt, founder of EST and Landmark Forum, Randy Revell, who founded Context Trainings, and Tom and Jane Willhite, founders of PSI World, to name just a few.

Jess Stern's book entitled The Power of Alpha Thinking gives a fascinating look at Alexander's work with Mind Dynamics and how it was viewed at the time.

Alexander, and many of those who have taken up his baton, teach a technique called Centering. In my experience it is a methodology that is effective for most people and can be learned and applied quickly, with, what can be, life changing results.

I consider Centering to be a bridge to a meditative state. It brings alpha brainwaves into easy reach for people who are willing to learn the basic technique and consistently use it. When we Centre, we use the power of our mind to create our life.

When we block our alpha mind we block the sun's light, and therefore our ability to reflect the light of who we are. We can have balance only when we have both our alpha and beta minds working. Most of us have highly developed beta minds. It is time to learn to develop our alpha minds.

As Jim Clemmer says in his book Growing the Distance:

"Centered leaders are continually exploring
inner space. They draw outward leadership
strength from their heart and soul."

Centering brings together breathing techniques, guided visualization and meditation to take us to alpha thinking, connecting us with our inner mind and the genius that resides there. It allows us to balance our four natures: physical, emotional, mental and spiritual or equivalently our four pillars: health, relationships, wealth and contribution.

The Spectrum Centering

The centering that is described and scripted in this chapter is the Spectrum Centering. It is based on the Rainbow Centering developed by Alexander Everett and set out in his book Inward Bound – Living Life from the Inside Out. Doug and I were fortunate to spend a week with Alexander at his retreat called Love, Life and Light in 1998. At that time, Alexander, who had known Doug for some time, gave us his blessing to take his centering material and use it as we saw fit.

The Spectrum Centering takes us through a process to relax our bodies, enrich our emotions, and calm, still and focus our minds so that we are able to release our true spirit and experience being centered people.

There is no right or wrong way to experience a centering, just trust the process and follow it through. Different people have different experiences. And the same person centering at different times will have different experiences.

Some people have a challenge with visualization. They find it very difficult to see a mental picture. That's OK. For some it is not a picture but a sense of something or a feeling that happens. Just stick with the process and practice. Whether you see a picture or not, results will come for you if you are getting to alpha thinking.

Centering can be used in a proactive way to generate images of the life you want and the feelings associated with those images. For example, you want a new car, then once you are centered you can visualize, in lots of detail, that new car. Equally importantly as the visual image, is that you feel how it would feel for you to have that car. How about a situation where you want to change the dynamics of a relationship with someone you know? Visualize the relationship as you want it to be and feel the feelings of that relationship as you want it to be.

Centering is an experience involving all your senses and all four pillars. Since it is experiential in nature, centering is best learned in an experiential setting: a coaching session, a workshop. Also, a different power and energy is often achieved when a group of people centre together. That being said, some learning about centering and any opportunity to put it into practice is better than none. Therefore, I am going to describe, in detail, the basic Full Spectrum centering methodology and at the end of the chapter provide a script for you to get started with centering. Please get in touch with me if you would like to have the benefit of an experiential session with me to learn centering.

The Spectrum Centering process uses the colours of the spectrum. The process takes you down through the seven colours to your centre. Once you are there, you can either, just rest quietly in that centered space and allow whatever comes up for you to emerge, or, you can use visualization to create something in your life. It may be about any of your four pillars: health, wealth, relationships or contribution. After a period of time has passed, you then come back up through the colours in reverse sequence. Using a particular uplifting and joyful affirmation, which you will find at the end of the Centering script, you open your eyes and come back to the world.

I have experienced some marvelous journeys during my centering's. I have had eagles and other creatures and people supporting me as I journey. Other times, when I have just been quiet in my centered space, solutions to problems have come to me. I have used healing imagery in centering's. I have prepared for important presentations using visualization in centering's. I have prepared for dance exams. Just three weeks after I met Doug, I was centering with the intention of just sitting quietly in my centered space and not visualizing anything in particular, and there I saw myself marrying him. We weren't even dating! You just never know what might happen in your centered space and then in your life.

Red: I Relax my Body

Red is the physical relaxation colour. It is a well-proven fact that most disease is associated in some way with stress. We hold stress, tension and emotion in our physical body. As we relax the physical body we are able to start to let go of these stresses. For many people, their physical body is out of balance. It might be weight issues, health problems, tightness holding onto stress and emotion, lack of strength or stamina, or low energy. Does it affect the other parts of life when our physical nature is out of balance? As we use the colour red to relax our physical body we are also rebalancing, harmonising and energising our physical nature.

The first time you do the Spectrum Centering it is particularly advantageous to do a prolonged full body relaxation process from the top of the head to the toes. Focus your awareness on each part of your body one after the other. Breathe relaxation into every muscle and organ as you gradually work your way down your body. This will anchor the relaxation to the colour red for you so that in future you can short cut to physical relaxation using the colour red.

Orange: I Release my Emotions

Orange is the emotional colour. It is used to release and let go of the past. The key to life is to forgive. Forgiveness creates freedom for ourselves. Many people have a tough time with the emotional side of life. Could having the ability to release past hurts, anger and resentment be valuable? In the Centering process we use the colour orange to trigger the release of our emotions and focus on living our emotional life at a higher level. By focusing on the highest feeling that you can possibly have for your fellow man and woman and moving your awareness out of yourself into your fellow men and women, your feelings, emotions and desires become more still and at peace.

Yellow: I Calm and Still my Mind

Yellow is the mental relaxation colour. We use it to calm and still the mind. How powerful and liberating it is to have the ability to turn off the yap-yap voice in my head and cut through the confusing mental chatter. With a calm and focused mind answers come naturally from within.

One way of achieving a calm and still mind is to mentally go to a special place in nature. See yourself in this nature scene and surround yourself with the forces of nature. Use all your senses. Direct all of your attention, awareness and consciousness into nature. As you do this, you will find your mind becomes calm and still.

Another way is to imagine that your thoughts are clouds in a bright blue sky. At first the clouds are dashing across the sky as your mind works at a rapid pace. Put your awareness into slowing the clouds down. Gradually the clouds move slower and slower and become fewer and fewer. When a thought/cloud appears, just let it go. Don't follow it or give it any energy or attention. Let it go and soon you will be looking at clear blue sky with a calm and still mind.

Green: I Sense Peace Within

Green is the colour of peace. Do you have peace if you are upset, distressed, distracted? But peace is as natural as breathing. Our Natural state is not upset, distressed and distracted, it is peaceful. Do you want to live in peace? Would you like to have a greater sense of peace as you go through your daily life? Have you been frustrated in your attempts to achieve that? Being Centered is the key.

Now that you have relaxed your body physically, released your emotions and stilled your mind, you can enter the fourth state: peace. At this point we are moving into the inner mind, the spiritual part of our being. Feel and sense the peace within you. Peace is within every cell of your body.

As you connect with the peace that is a Natural part of you, your thoughts, feelings and behaviour can become more Natural, finding their source in the peace at your centre. You can also release peace from within and become a peaceful influence on everyone around you. By being centered and thereby being a peaceful influence, we change the world into a more peaceful place.

Blue: I Feel Love for Myself and Others

Blue is the colour of love. Love is our true nature. I love you and I accept you, even though I don't understand you. I love myself and I accept myself, even though I don't understand myself. Fear contaminates love. Using the colour blue, we develop our Natural ability to give and receive love. Once we relax the body, release the emotions, calm the mind and sense peace, then we can express love. Imagine love rises up and pours out of you. Let it flow out of every cell and pore of your body, so it may touch all of the people around you. Feel that you are full of love and giving love freely to all.

Purple: I Seek Out the Depths Within

Purple is the colour of aspiration. Once we experience peace and love, then we become a seeker. We seek the truth of who we really are and our purpose. The colour purple takes us to the inner most parts of our being: the core and essence of who we really are. The place where we *know*.

Violet: I Am Centered

The seventh and final colour of the spectrum is violet. Violet represents the innermost core of our being. This is where we are centered. As you use the colour violet, feel that you are now there deep within the inner part of your being. This is where you become more self-realized, and better know who you really are. When you are connected to the violet centre, you know the truth about yourself and your purpose.

Spectrum Centering Script

The following is a script to use to Centre yourself. The ideal is to Centre for 15 minutes in the morning and 15 minutes in the evening, every day. If that is too much of a stretch, do whatever you can. Something is better than nothing.

You may wish to record yourself speaking the script and play it when you Centre so that you can focus on getting centered rather than on what words to tell yourself. Having some gentle instrumental music playing quietly in the background can enhance the Centering.

"I now prepare to centre myself and become more aware of my inner being.

I close my eyes for peace and quiet. I straighten my spine to stimulate energy flow. I open my hands to receive and I just let go and relax. Relax. Relax. Relax.

My breathing is slow and peaceful. I can feel my body becoming more and more relaxed with each breath that I take.

As I take a deep breath now and slowly exhale, I visualize something red from nature. A red flower. A red fruit. Red is my physical relaxation colour. As I see this colour red in my mind's eye, I relax my body from head to foot. I feel a wave of relaxation moving downward through my body. And I bring my body into a complete state of relaxation.

Relax. Relax. Relax. I let go of my body and I just relax.

Next, as I take another deep breath and slowly exhale, I visualize something orange from nature. I choose a fruit, a vegetable or a flower that is orange. Orange is my emotional release colour. As I see the colour orange clearly in my mind's eye, I release and let go of my emotions. I neither dramatise nor deny my feelings. I desire only that which is good for myself and others.

As I move down the spectrum to yellow, I take another deep breath and slowly exhale, and I visualize something yellow from nature. I visualize a yellow fruit or flower, or maybe the sun itself. Yellow is my mental relaxation colour. As I see the colour yellow clearly in my mind's eye, I calm and still my mind. I bring my mind to rest. I find that when I calm and still my mind, answers come to me naturally from within.

As I relax and go deeper still.

Next, as I take another deep breath and slowly exhale, I visualize something green from nature. I see some green grass or trees. As I see the colour green clearly in my mind's eye, I sense a state of peacefulness within. Green is the colour of peace. And peace is now able to fill my life. I feel myself filled with peace. I allow peace to permeate my entire being.

Peace. Peace. Peace.

I sense that indwelling presence of peace. This peace is always there. And I can experience it whenever I relax my body, release my emotions and calm my mind.

Next, as I take another deep breath and slowly exhale, I move down the spectrum to blue. I visualize something blue from nature. As I see the colour blue clearly in my mind's eye, I feel myself full of love. I feel love moving to me and through me to others as if I am a living conduit for love.

I always remember, love in my heart wasn't put there to stay, love isn't love until I give it away.

Next, as I take another deep breath and slowly exhale, I visualize something purple from nature. I choose a purple fruit or flower. Purple is the colour for aspiration, for seeking the truth. As I see the colour purple clearly in my mind's eye, I aspire to that inner secret place. I seek out the depths within. I desire to find and fulfil my life purpose. And know that I will make a positive difference within my life.

As I take another deep breath and slowly exhale, I visualize something violet from nature. As I see this inner most colour violet clearly in my mind's eye, I enter the inner most part of my being.

I am now there.

I am centered.

I am now at one with myself. A state that encompasses all of time. I just become aware of the totality of the now. Only conscious of the present. I feel and sense this one moment in time. I am at one with my inner self. I am calm. I am still. I am at peace. I am centered."

This is the space for you to spend a few minutes centered.

Use guided visualization to create results you wish to see in your life. Or you can just be still and allow whatever needs to emerge to come forth.

"I now prepare to return to the everyday world. And I come back slowly from the centre of my being. From the inner to the outer.

I remember, that after centering myself, spiritually I become more enlightened. In fact, my inner light shines so brightly that it affects all of those in my world in a positive manner. This is turn affects me mentally. And I become more enriched, my thoughts more pure and creative. Which affects me emotionally and I become more enthusiastic. My feelings will be more loving and kind. Which affects me physically and I become more energized with the fullness of life.

For after centering myself I know that with my inner spiritual power all things are possible in my life. And that whatever the spirit within leads me to do, I will do better than ever before.

In fact, each day, in every way, I am getting better and better and better.

Now in a few moments I need to open my eyes. So I prepare to visualize the colours of the spectrum in reverse sequence. Starting with that inner most colour violet. Moving upward and out to purple. Then further up to blue. Next green. Then yellow, orange and red. I open my eyes and I am wide awake.

Revitalized, refreshed and in tune with life.

I am enlightened, I am enriched, I am enthused, I am energized.

I just am. I just am."

Chapter 10: The Power of The Mind

One of the recurring themes that you will, by now, be starting to recognize is the subject of choice. One of the traits that make human beings different from the rest of the animal kingdom is the ability to make choices.

We can choose to develop and grow or we can choose to remain as we are. We can choose how we respond to situations and people. We can choose to look on the bright side or find the negative in a circumstance. We can choose to respond from the present or allow our old habits and programmes to steer our lives. We can choose to take charge of our lives or we can abdicate that choice. And so it goes on. We can choose how we live our life.

As Og Mandino said in his book The Choice,

> *"Every day all of us make hundreds of choices,*
> *most of them so menial and habitual that they*
> *are almost as automatic as breathing. Those*
> *who live in unhappy failure have never*
> *exercised their options for the better things of*
> *life because they have never been aware that*
> *they had any choices."*

Sometimes it is not easy to recognize that there are choices in front of us. Sometimes we are surrounded by others who don't recognize that there are choices. If they are experts, or advisors, it takes courage and determination to halt their process and stop to make a conscious choice. Perhaps you end up doing what they are advising, but it is from a place of conscious choice on your part, rather than a feeling of having no choice but to take that direction.

Let me give you an example. In the evening of Thursday March 17th 2011, Doug was admitted to hospital after a CT scan on his head revealed a 6cm tumour at the front of his brain. It was affecting his cognitive abilities to the extent that he was not capable of making his own decisions. It was not clear whether this was a piece of the original tumour that had regrown or whether this was a metastasized tumour. The neurosurgeon saw him the next day and then spoke to me.

He said he was prepared to operate. He would clear the operating room schedule for Monday and remove the tumour. I could tell that he expected me to thank him profusely and let his process roll forward without a second thought. However, even in that situation of extreme stress, I recognized that there was a choice to be made. Instead of submitting to the "expert's" plan, I started to ask questions. If this surgery was to go ahead, it would be by conscious choice.

Let's back track a few months here. After Doug had the first tumour removed from his olfactory nerve and up into his brain, the surgeon advised that he have some radiation treatment "just to be sure". Once cleared after his surgery, we started down that route. Doug was scanned every which way and there was no sign of any cancer anywhere else in his body. The radiation oncologists planned their approach in great detail and then we met with the man who would oversee his treatment. At that point he told us the plan, the "for sure" damage and the risks for things to go wrong.

For Doug, the logic fell apart when the doctor said that, because of the location, they would have to use "compromised dosages". When pushed, the oncologist translated that for us as meaning that they knew they needed to give him x dosage to be sure they got the job done, but in fact would only be able to give him less than x, otherwise they would destroy too much of his brain. We went away and considered the options, even though we could tell the attitude of the oncologist was that there were no options.

Doug chose not to have radiation. Instead he went to an integrative medical institute for a month to undertake a range of therapies to build up his natural ability to deal with cancer rather than go through a process of destruction, "just in case", that would, if all went well, have some major quality of life implications for the rest of his life, and could result in catastrophic damage, with doses that were insufficient to be sure that the cancer was destroyed. The oncologists were taken aback that Doug actually felt that he had a choice.

Fast forward five months, back to the conversation with the neurosurgeon. He is assuming he is going to operate on Doug's brain in three days to remove a large tumour. I asked what the likely outcome would look like in terms of Doug's capabilities. Silence. I acknowledged that he could not make any forecast with certainty, but asked him to talk to me in terms of probabilities... I understand that way of thinking. Silence. I asked what was the best possible outcome from the surgery. Finally I got a response! He said that, at best, they would stabilize Doug's capabilities as they were at the time of the surgery for a while and that then, over the next two to three years, he would decline and die. OK. Now I have something I can work with! Then I said, "I presume that with this type of surgery there are a lot of things that can go wrong including the fact that he might die on the table, or shortly afterwards as a result of bleeds or infection." He grunted, which I took to be agreement.

Then I said, "And what about other options. What do the outcomes look like?" Silence. Long silence. So I said, "There is always at least one other option. We can choose to do nothing." Silence. "What does it look like if we choose to do nothing?" Pause. And finally a response. He said he would decline and die over the next 8 to 12 weeks.

This decision was to be mine to make because of Doug's impaired cognitive ability. Fortunately, he had a living will and he had shown me the way by his own choice not to do radiation therapy. When I thanked the neurosurgeon the next day but informed him that Doug would not be going through the surgery, I was greeted once again by silence and an attitude of incredulity that I even thought there was a decision to make.

It was actually 8 weeks to the day that Doug died peacefully, bravely, with no pain and in total acceptance. He had continued to take full responsibility for his own life experience up to his last breath.

THERE IS ALWAYS A CHOICE.

Our lives are a succession of choices moment by moment. Some choices are extreme like the examples I have just given. Others seem minute, almost irrelevant, and yet those seemingly tiny choices we make moment by moment determine the quality of our life experience.

The key is to recognise that every moment we have a choice about our thoughts, our feelings and our behavior and to exercise that choice, rather than living unconsciously or at the bidding of those around us.

A Model of Choice and Accountability

This model of choice and accountability helps to delve into The Responsibility Principle: I and I alone, am 100% responsible for my entire life experience.

We have seen in the discussion of The Responsibility Principle in Chapter 3, that it is not the circumstances that determine our life experience. It is how we view those circumstances.

We can choose to be a victim of circumstance, or accountable for the results in our lives. We all have circumstances in our lives. Everyone has got their "stuff", past or present, they are dealing with. Each of us individually chooses how we view our circumstances.

The diagram below summarises the choices we face day in and day out, moment by moment. It shows the cycle of a victim of circumstance and the cycle of someone accountable for their results.

We can see people or circumstances as a threat and react negatively putting us on the first step in the victim cycle. Or we can view people and circumstances as an opportunity and pro-act positively.

If we view the circumstance as a threat, we react. The emotions that come up are then negative. As are the behaviours. We become dysfunctional, angry, defensive, immature, Normal. If we do it long enough, we become a Victim of Circumstance and are in the no growth cycle.

If we view the circumstance as an opportunity we become pro-active. We get excited. Our behaviour becomes creative, successful, positive, Natural. We start to become Accountable for our Results and are in the growth cycle. We become more and more accountable for the way that we think, the way we feel and the way we behave.

It takes skill and awareness. It takes living consciously. Looking for the choices. Noticing the choices. And having the courage to evaluate the choices, even in circumstances where those around you are taking the approach that there are no choices. This is not one of those concepts where all of a sudden you are perfect at being accountable for results. Choice is so all pervasive in our lives, that there will always be an opportunity to take your accountability to another level. It is about practice and an intention to live more accountably day by day.

Accountability

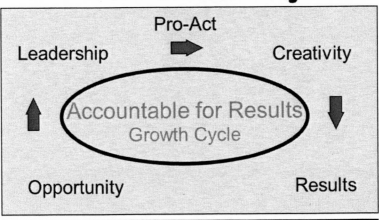

Pro-Act

Leadership ➡ Creativity

⬆ **Accountable for Results**
Growth Cycle ⬇

Opportunity   Results

+
The Circumstances of Life
It is how I view my circumstances that is important
–

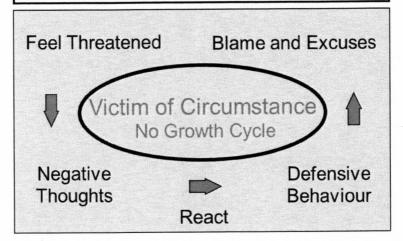

Feel Threatened   Blame and Excuses

⬇ **Victim of Circumstance**
No Growth Cycle ⬆

Negative
Thoughts ➡ Defensive
Behaviour

React

Let's finish this chapter with a short story that Doug used to tell to illustrate the point.

There was a pair of identical twin boys. One had a negative view of circumstances. The other took a positive view. One day, the negative boy was shut in a room full of toys. The researchers observe him as he destroys the toys and they find him very unhappy at the end of the process. The positive boy is placed in room full of manure. The researchers watch him cheerfully digging in the manure. When they ask him what he is doing, he happily replies that he is looking for the pony!

It is not the circumstance that counts. It is how you view it. Do you have a choice?

Chapter 11: Responsibility in Relationships

Given that one of the two overarching principles of a Full Spectrum Life and living life at a higher level is The Responsibility Principle, responsibility is clearly an important element to explore, understand and apply in life. Let's remind ourselves of The Responsibility Principle:

I, and I alone, am 100% responsible for my
entire life experience.

Remember, the emphasis is on life *experience* not life *circumstance*. The two are totally different. What defines my life experience is the way that I think, the way that I feel and the way that I behave.

In the previous chapter we saw how accountability and choice are interlinked and the consequences of choosing to view circumstances in a negative light versus a positive light. That initial choice of perspective leads, either to being accountable for your results in a growth cycle, or being a victim of circumstances in a no growth cycle. The Responsibility Principle states that you and you alone are responsible for that choice of perspective and its ensuing consequences.

We are now going to focus on the role of responsibility in the quality of our relationships. Doug used to say:

"Responsibility is probably the single most
important concept in relationships. And
certainly the most misunderstood."

This chapter presents a model of responsibility that provides a framework within which to view your relationships. The more deeply you apply the Full Spectrum Responsibility Model in your life, the more the quality and effectiveness of your relationships will be enhanced. Guaranteed.

How about we start with the Oxford English Dictionary definition of responsibility.

1. *The state or fact of having a duty to deal with something or of having control over someone.*
2. *The state or fact of being accountable or to blame for something.*
3. *A moral obligation to behave correctly towards or in respect of.*

These definitions give us a clue into an important distinction that the Full Spectrum Responsibility Model encapsulates, namely: there are things that we are **responsible for** and there are things that we have **responsibility towards**.

Understanding the difference between responsible for and responsible to is a foundation for the successful application of the Full Spectrum Responsibility Model in your relationships.

Responsibility For and Responsibility To
The first part of the Full Spectrum Responsibility Model is the distinction between what and who I am responsible for and what and who I am responsible to.

- I am responsible *for* myself, and no one else. I am responsible for the way that I think, the way that I feel and the way that I behave. I am responsible for **MY** thoughts, **MY** feelings and **MY** actions.

- I am responsible *to* others. To love them, to empower them, to inspire them, to guide them, to support them emotionally, to treat them with dignity and respect. But I am *not* responsible for making their decisions and choices for them or for the way that they think, feel or behave.

The responsibility for and responsibility to statements are short, clear and simple. And yet they belie a multitude of layers of complexity that will gradually reveal themselves to you as you start to apply this in your life. Understanding and applying these statements can relieve you of otherwise impossible burdens in relationships. You will be set free by using these statements as your guide.

Having lived with Doug through the ups and downs of depression, I can tell you from my own experience what a weight was lifted from my shoulders when I really started to "get" the fact that I was not responsible for how he was feeling. I was only responsible to treat him kindly, gently, lovingly, respectfully, with acceptance and do everything I could to make the environment one in which he could be happy. But when he still had a down period, I finally realised that I was not responsible for that, having done all I could do to be responsible to him. I can also tell you from my experience that I understand how difficult it is to let go of feeling responsible for their feelings in those closest and dearest of relationships. But I encourage you to free yourself by taking on board this distinction between responsible for and responsible to.

Responsibility and Irresponsibility

The second part of the Full Spectrum Responsibility Model is the following:

- When I am responsible *for myself*, then and only then, can I be responsible *to others*.

If I am irresponsible for myself, i.e. I am not being responsible for my own thoughts, feelings and actions, then I cannot be responsible to others. I am automatically irresponsible to others, if only in terms of placing the responsibility for my thoughts, feelings and action on them. But likely also in many other ways.

What does irresponsibility to others look like? Basically any kind of dysfunctionality, discomfort or dissatisfaction in a relationship comes down to irresponsibility. Either you are being irresponsible for your own thoughts, feelings and actions and thereby placing responsibility on others and hence putting them in a position of irresponsibility to you, or you are trying to take responsibility for other people's thoughts, feelings and actions, including making their decisions and choices for them.

This is not just about intimate relationships, or even about wider personal relationships. Exactly the same applies in professional relationships. Have you ever worked for someone who would not let you get on with doing your work? They try to take over, micro manage the process or even do it themselves. Were they being responsible to you or irresponsible to you? Contrast that with working for someone who teaches you, guides you, empowers you, supports you and is there as a resource for you. Which is the most successful working relationship? Which is the most effective from the standpoint of productivity and quality as well?

The Full Spectrum Responsibility Model

Pulling it all together, here is the diagrammatic representation of the Full Spectrum Responsibility Model.

	For Myself	**To Others**	
Responsible	I am responsible FOR myself: for my thoughts, for my feelings, for my behaviours.	I am responsible TO others: to love, to support, to inspire.	**Responsible**
Irresponsible	I am irresponsible for myself when I let others take responsibility for my thoughts, for my feelings, for my behaviours.	I am irresponsible to others when I take responsibility for others' thoughts, for others' feelings, for others' behaviours	**Irresponsible**
	For Myself	**To Others**	

The relationship between parents and children can get very messy when it comes to responsibility. Where does children's responsibility for themselves begin and parents responsibility shift from responsible for to responsible to with their children? When children are young they rely on those parenting them for everything. As a parent, therefore, we are responsible to our children to feed, clothe and provide a home for them… but only as is appropriate for their age. At some point the responsibility to feed, clothe and house them becomes part of what a child is responsible for themselves. Does it serve the child or the parents to continue providing for them well beyond the point at which they are capable of doing it themselves? Does it serve the child or the parents' to continually bail out a child that has not learned good money management? At what point does the child need to be empowered to make its own decisions about things like subjects to study, career paths, friends, partner's?

None of the answers to these and the many other questions that arise around responsibility in the relationship between parents and children are straight forward or clearly defined. However, we have found that, considering these questions in the context of the Full Spectrum Responsibility Model provides tremendous insight and more clarity than trying to consider them without the help of this tool.

The situations in which the Full Spectrum Responsibility Model can provide useful insight and help in making choices are so varied and infinite in number. If you dig deeply enough you will find that any difficulty in a relationship can be traced back to one of the parties in the relationship starting down the irresponsibility route. Codependent relationships are clear examples of relationships where both parties are being irresponsible for themselves and, therefore, irresponsible to each other.

The nuances of the application of the model to relationships of all kinds are subtle and there will always be a higher level to which you can take your understanding and use of the model. There are layers within layers of ever deepening understanding to be had as you use this tool in your life.

Addiction is an example of one of the challenging situations in which responsibility for and to and irresponsibility plays an important role. Clearly, the addict is not being responsible to themselves. That is a fact not a judgment. Since they are not responsible for themselves, they cannot be responsible to others. That irresponsibility to others may be across a wide spectrum from being physically, mentally and emotionally abusive to those around them, to stealing to pay for an addiction, to absenteeism or diverting family funds to the addiction.

The challenging part comes when we put ourselves in the shoes of the people around the addict: spouse, family, friends, coworkers. How many times should parents pay their grown child's rent or mortgage because they have spent their money on alcohol, drugs, gambling or whatever is their particular addiction? Same question for a sibling, a friend, a partner. How many times should a coworker cover for the addict's absenteeism or inability to perform their work? How many times should a family make excuses for one of its members' behavior? How many times should a family not make social plans just in case the addict is out of control that day?

Bottom line: how can the people around an addict be responsible for themselves and to the addict? Is empowering them in their addiction by covering for them, bailing them out, making excuses for them, and putting up a façade for the outside world being responsible to them? It is a complex and heart breaking situation to deal with. Those around the addict need access to professional help, such as AL Anon, just as the addict needs professional help when they are ready to seek it. Looking at the situation from the perspective of responsibility and irresponsibility is one helpful tool that can start the journey towards healing those around the addict.

Because the nuances of responsibility and irresponsibility are so subtle as you go deeper, the lines between responsibility for and to and the distinction between responsibility and irresponsibility are not always crystal clear. However, what you will find, as you assess your relationships within the framework of the Full Spectrum Responsibility Model, is that you gain much more insight and clarity than stumbling on blindly without this way of looking at what is going on. Always remember the first step of the five steps to growth: "Hot dog, I got some confusion!"

Whenever you feel some discomfort or dysfunctionality in a relationship, when you find yourself getting uncentered about a person, whether that is a friend, a loved one, a family member or a professional contact, ask yourself, "How am I being irresponsible in this relationship? And what do I need to do to become responsible for myself and responsible to them?"

When dealing with particularly dysfunctional relationships, I have found the following question very useful to help to clarify how I might be able to be more responsible to them and less responsible for them:

Does this act that I am considering reinforce
them in their dysfunctionality or move them
towards being responsible for themselves?

When we try to take responsibility for others, what does it do to the love and the trust? It always destroys it. There is no question in my mind that, when people understand the responsibility model and its implications for the quality of their relationships, they want to live being responsible for themselves and to others. This can only happen with any consistency by being centered.

Responsibility Journaling Exercise
To enable you to get more clarity on how responsibility and irresponsibility has played out in your own life, here is a series of questions for you to use to journal your insights around the Full Spectrum Responsibility Model.

1. Who has taken responsibility for you, and how has that created resentment in your life?
2. Who have you taken responsibility for and how has that created resentment in your life?
3. How have you been irresponsible for yourself, and how has that affected how you are living?
4. Who have you been irresponsible to, and how has that affected the relationship?
5. How important is it for you to become more responsible for yourself?

Chapter 12: Forgiveness

Forgiveness is a pivotal part of personal development and finding the way to living in peace and balance. However, there is only so much that you can get from reading about forgiveness. The real breakthroughs come when you *experience* forgiveness.

As a starting point though, it is important to learn about the focus of forgiveness, what it is, what it is not and a process for forgiveness. This we can do in the written word. After that, you will need to experience forgiveness by putting into practice these words in order to really learn the lessons that forgiveness brings and to accumulate the benefits of forgiveness in your life.

Jack Kornfield, teacher and writer on Buddhist Psychology says:

"Forgiveness is an honourable practice."

The key here being that it is a practice. This is not about theory or philosophy. It is about practice, the way we live, about making our life better.

There are two perspectives on forgiveness, the perspective of the person doing the forgiving and the perspective of the person being forgiven. Whilst many of the major world religions have a focus on forgiveness, in many cases it is about us being forgiven by the deity (ies). Since this is a book about personal development, our concern here is not about us being forgiven by others, but about us doing the forgiving. After all, we have no control over whether someone else will forgive us. We can only control ourselves being forgiving.

Let's start with a definition of forgive from the Oxford English Dictionary:

• *Stop feeling angry or resentful towards (someone) for an offence, flaw, or mistake.*

There is growing scientific research evidence that people who are angry and hold resentments are unhappier than those who don't and, in addition, they live shorter lives with less quality of life.

Forgiveness is the process that frees us from anger and resentment. It changes our life today as we are freed from the unpleasant feelings of anger and resentment. And it changes our life in the future as we let go of the long term impacts on our wellbeing. Forgiveness is a choice about the way that we think, the way that we feel and the way that we behave. It is an application of The Responsibility Principle and model. In some cases, it is a choice between life and death.

When Doug introduced the section on forgiveness in his workshops, he would emphasise how pivotal a time the next part of the class could be for everyone there. He would tell the participants how it was the understanding and experience of forgiveness that he gained in a workshop with Jim Quinn that literally saved his life and gave him the opportunity to become the man he became.

Doug endured a tragic childhood, youth and early adulthood. He would tell of how, by the time he was four years old he was on his fourth mother. His adoptive father was physically and emotionally abusive. He was sexually abused by someone outside the family. He suffered from depression from the age of 3. He became an alcoholic and drug addict as a youth. He lived on the streets of Toronto at the age of 15. Later at around 30, when his son was just 4 months old his young wife took his son away from Canada where Doug was not able to get any rights to see him.

Doug would say that, at the point that he came across Jim Quinn and his experiential trainings, he had lost all hope of his life ever being anything but suffering. He was still a practicing alcoholic the first time he experienced the Forgiveness Process. It was during this exercise that he saw a glimmer of hope that his life could be different. It could be better. It was a year later that he took his last drink, but he credits the Forgiveness Cycle that Saturday afternoon as the moment when the last drink became possible. And with that last drink came the opportunity for him to become the magnificent human being that I later met and married.

Forgiveness was a practice for Doug. He recognized the need to consistently practice forgiveness and that there were layers within layers of work to do to free himself from his past and then to blossom into who he really was. The following quote sums up what forgiveness is about. It is attributed to Landrum Bolling, peace activist:

> *"Forgiveness means giving up all hope of a better past."*

Doug is an extreme example. But forgiveness can change your life for the better too. Forgiveness is your chance to free yourself.

What is Forgiveness?

Forgiveness, like many spiritual practices, is in some ways a selfish thing to do. Forgiveness is a choice. Forgiveness is not about the other person. It is all about me. Why is that important? What if the person you need to forgive to free yourself from resentment is dead? What if the person you need to forgive doesn't give two hoots about whether you forgive them or not? **Forgiveness is not about the other person.** You forgive someone to free yourself. Fortunately, the process of forgiveness does not involve the other person at all. So you can do it without their involvement.

Forgiveness does not condone the behavior. Part of the process for forgiveness is to separate the behavior from the person. It is the person, the human being in all their own suffering and dysfunctionality that you forgive, not the behavior. Forgiving your abuser does not in any way make it OK that they abused you. It does, however, free you from anger, resentment, depression, fearfulness and all the other impacts that you are living as a result of not forgiving and letting go. It frees you to no longer be a victimized person. It gives you back your power.

Forgiveness does not necessarily result in reconciliation. Just because you have forgiven someone that is still alive, doesn't mean to say that you have to have a relationship with them, or go back to the same form of relationship that you had with them. Forgiveness is a strong and courageous stance. It allows you to protect yourself from further harm by not engaging in a toxic or abusive relationship whilst being free of anger and resentment.

Perhaps the hardest person of all to forgive, and so perhaps the most important of all, is ourself. Yes, we need to forgive others who have hurt us and caused us to hold anger and resentment. But we also need to forgive ourselves.

The kinds of things we need to forgive ourselves for include giving up on ourselves or our dreams, hurting other people, beating up on ourselves, reacting negatively to people or situations, not standing up for ourselves, betraying someone... Anything we are not proud of or has caused us pain, anger, guilt or any other negative emotion.

Sometimes it can sound irrational. "Why should I forgive myself for not being there to support my parents because I became ill? I couldn't help being ill." But if you are feeling guilt, or any other negative emotion connected with it, then yes you need to forgive yourself.

Robert Enright, Professor of Educational Psychology at the University of Wisconsin-Madison developed a four phase process of forgiveness. He has written extensively on forgiveness, including co-authoring the book Exploring Forgiveness with Archbishop Desmond Tutu and Joanna North. His process of forgiveness is made up as follows:

1. Uncovering Phase: in which a person gains insight into whether and how the injustice and subsequent injury have compromised his or her life.
2. Decision Phase: in which a person gains an accurate understanding of the nature of forgiveness and makes a decision to commit to forgiving on the basis of this understanding.
3. Work Phase: in which a person reframes their view of the offender and starts to see them as a human being rather than evil incarnate.

4. Deepening Phase: in which a person begins to find new meaning in their experience of suffering and finds release from the "emotional prison" of anger and resentment.

Forgiveness Process

Though it was designed long before Robert Enright expounded his four phases to achieve forgiveness, the Full Spectrum Forgiveness Cycle encompasses all the elements of Enright's model. It is designed, and is at its most powerful, as an experiential exercise. However, I will translate it into a journaling exercise for you here.

Whether undertaken as a journaling exercise as set out here, or done as an experiential process in a class, this is a private exercise. The class is set up in such a way to ensure that even, though a group of participants is going through the process all at the same time, each person has their privacy.

This journaling process can be used to forgive people from your past, people currently in your life and yourself. Each person is worked on individually. It is advisable to do this journaling process in a place where you have privacy.

For each person there are three steps to go through. First you will unleash your feelings about what they did to you. You will really let them know what they did to you and how it made you feel. You will release the anger and resentment you have been holding towards them. Next you will start to look at them in a different way, separating their behavior from them, the person. And thirdly, you will use Formula A to deal with them in a different way and bring yourself to a loving and accepting place of peace.

Forgiveness Process for Someone from the Past or Present

1. It is vitally important that you first of all centre yourself.

2. Now imagine someone from your past or presently in your life that you need to forgive. Someone that has caused you pain, anger, sorrow, shame, resentment. See them standing in front of you.

3. Start to write in your journal. Don't worry about sentence construction or grammar. Just let your feelings out. Tell them what they did, how it made you feel, the effect it has had on your life. Tell them about the pain, the sorrow, the anger, the guilt, the resentment. Let it out onto the paper as you imagine them standing in front of you.

4. After a few minutes of unloading yourself it will be time to stop and see if you can see them in a different way. Imagine them in front of you again. Look deeply into their eyes. Do you see their hurt, their pain, their sorrow, their unfulfilled dreams, their fear? Now imagine them as a small child. Did they get the love and the nurturing they needed? Did they experience hurt and suffering of some kind? Write down what pain, fear and hurt you see in them.

5. Use Formula A to reinforce the separation of the behavior from the person and to bring yourself to a place of love, acceptance and forgiveness. Write it down. Say it out loud. "I love you and I accept you, even though I don't understand you." And now add, "And I forgive you". Repeat until you can *feel* love, acceptance and forgiveness.

6. Then release this person. See them once again in their adult form and wish them well in their life.

7. Close your eyes. Spend a few minutes quietly centered in this feeling of love, acceptance and forgiveness.

8. Gently bring yourself back up through the colours out of your centering and back to your present time and place.

Forgiveness Process for Yourself

1. It is vitally important that you first of all centre yourself.

2. See yourself standing in front of you. We are going to look at ourselves and our own behavior and how we have caused ourselves pain and anger.

3. Start to write in your journal. Don't worry about sentence construction or grammar. Just let your feelings out. Tell yourself what you did, how it made you feel, the effect it has had on your life. Really unload on yourself for every time you have given up on yourself, sabotaged yourself or done something you are not proud of. Tell yourself about the pain, the sorrow, the anger, the guilt, the resentment. Let it out onto the paper as you imagine yourself standing in front of you.

4. After a few minutes of unloading yourself it will be time to stop and see if you can see yourself in a different way. Imagine yourself in front of you again. Look deeply into your eyes. Do you see the hurt, the pain, the sorrow, the unfulfilled dreams, the fear? Now imagine yourself as a small child. Did you get the love and the nurturing you needed? Did you experience hurt and suffering of some

kind? Write down what pain, fear and hurt you see in yourself.

5. Use Formula A to reinforce the separation of the behavior from the person and to bring yourself to a place of love, acceptance and forgiveness. Write it down. Say it out loud. "I love myself and I accept myself, even though I don't understand myself." And now add, "And I forgive myself". Repeat until you can *feel* love, acceptance and forgiveness.

6. Then release yourself.

7. Close your eyes. Spend a few minutes quietly centered in this feeling of love, acceptance and forgiveness.

8. Gently bring yourself back up through the colours out of your centering and back to your present time and place.

Repeat the Forgiveness Process regularly to take your life to higher and higher levels.

Chapter 13: The Road of Life

As we start to bring all of these concepts together, let me share a funny little model with you that may shed light on the way you have been living and what you might want to do to start living life at a higher level. Comical as this model may seem, the insights can be profound. The model is called The Road of Life.

The Road of Life

Here is the Road of Life. Can there be some detours and bumps that throw us as we travel along the road of life? Whether we are trundling or racing, the bumps, sharp bends and detours can cause us to brake hard and throw us off course.

There are different types of house along the Road of Life. The first kind of house is a Problem House. When we get out on the Road of Life do we sometimes run into problems? When we do, we spend time in the Problem House. Have you ever spent time in the Problem House? The question is not whether life will involve time in the Problem House, but rather how long you stay there. We need to be in the Problem House long enough to see the problem. With awareness of the problem comes the opportunity to solve it.

How many get in to the Problem House and lock the door? You may have even dug a basement and sat down there, hiding out in the dark.

Sometimes we get so stuck in the Problem House that we build an R&D annex where we carry out Research and Development of problems. Have you ever found yourself in there, looking for more problems in life?

The second type of house on the Road of Life is a Cause House. This is where we look for the causes of our problems. How long do we want to stay in the Cause House? Long enough to see what the cause of the problem is and what it is doing to us. Without looking for the cause of our problems, any solutions will be like treating symptoms rather than dealing with the underlying cause of the problem.

But can we get stuck in the Cause House? Some people become cause archeologists. They dig and they dig. Then they dig some more thinking, "I just know there's got to be more down there!"

Some people dig a tunnel from the Cause House to the Problem House. Then they get trapped going back and forth, back and forth between the Problem House and the Cause House.

The third type of house is a Solution House. Here is where we look for solutions. We become solution oriented. How long do we want to stay here? Long enough to get a solution and get back on the Road of Life.

This book is about solutions you can access in the Solution House.

- The Commitment Principle
- The Responsibility Principle
- Strengthening and balancing the Four Pillars
- The opposing forces to fear reactions
- Formula A
- Centering
- Forgiveness
- Accountability and choice
- The Full Spectrum Responsibility Model

Of course there are many more sources of solutions available in the Solution House. This list just gives you an idea of what is available from a single approach and book. These work and they are part of a consistent framework and set of principles.

There is even a fourth type of house on the Road of Life. It is a mobile home. Do you know anybody who drags their problems through life? They keep making the same mistakes in life, driving over the same bumps in the road weighed down, slowed down and dragged down by the mobile home full of their past. They live in their mobile home taking their luggage everywhere with them.

Win-Win Solutions

Solutions that come out of the Full Spectrum Solution House are win-win solutions, i.e. the solutions are good for all those affected. In the words of John Denver, in his song It's About Time, "Who's to say you have to lose for someone else to win." Stephen Covey also places emphasis on win-win solutions. Habit #4 in his book The 7 Habits of Highly Effective People is "Think Win-Win".

No one has to lose. I don't have to lose. You don't have to lose. We can find solutions where we are both in a win situation. In fact, if we are applying the Full Spectrum Responsibility Model, then win-win are the only acceptable solutions. Only win-win solutions allow me to be responsible for myself and to others. Win-lose, lose-win or lose-lose means irresponsibility has crept in.

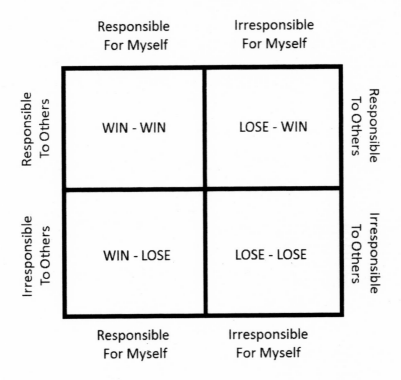

Finding win-win solutions often requires creativity. And where does our creativity reside? At the inner part of our mind. The part of our mind that we access through centering.

The third step in the five steps to growth model is incubation. The solutions that come at the illumination step are much more likely to be win-win if we have used centering as part of the incubation phase so that we are accessing our creative genius as we develop solutions.

Co-operation rather than competition is also often a key element in coming up with win-win solutions. Are we more likely to co-operate when we are living by Formula A or when we are living by Formula B?

Doug used to tell a story to illustrate a win-win solution in the world of finance and commodities.

"There had been a poor orange harvest due to bad weather. This resulted in a shortage of oranges on the commodities market. A new batch of oranges came onto the market one day and there were two bidders in particular going after this batch of oranges. They were bidding the price higher and higher, both parties wanting to win the deal and get the oranges. One of the brokers in the trading room figured out what was going on. He knew both of the companies bidding for the oranges. One of them was a juice company. They only wanted the pulp of the oranges. The other was a company making vaccines. They only needed the rind of the oranges. He was able to broker a solution through co-operation rather than competition. Both companies got what they needed, instead of one of them having to lose. The sellers of the oranges got a good price for their crop. It was win-win-win."

If you are living a Full Spectrum Life then you are always looking for win-win solutions. As you implement more and more win-win solutions in your life, then you will be living life at a higher and higher level.

Win-win solutions operate at the personal, family, neighbourhood, city, region, country, corporate, government, NGO and global level. There are no exceptions. Win-win is always the way to go in relationships.

Chapter 14: Proactive Visionary or Fear Based Reactionary? It's Your Choice.

The recognition of proactivity as a trait of highly effective people came out of the work of Victor Frankl. In his book The 7 habits of Highly Effective People, Stephen Covey describes his interpretation of proactivity and proactive people. In fact, "Be Proactive" is Stephen Covey's Habit #1. His description of proactivity is powerful, useful and fits the Full Spectrum principles. I will, therefore, quote it here:

> *"[Proactivity] means more than merely taking initiative. It means that as human beings, we are responsible for our own lives. Our behavior is a function of our decisions, not our conditions. We can subordinate feelings to values. We have the initiative and the responsibility to make things happen."*

In that definition you will see The Responsibility Principle, the emphasis on choice of our response to circumstances, and the importance of values, which translates to being centered and living from the I AM as a driver, rather than feelings.

It is worth talking about the role of feelings for a proactive person here. A proactive visionary realises that they were not given feelings to not have them, nor were they given feelings to become them. They were given feelings to interpret their environment in order to provide information as part of the decision making process. I feel excitement at the prospect of an opportunity and yet scared to warn me that caution may be required. But the feelings are only one input to my choice.

As a proactive visionary, my choices are not made by my feelings, rather I notice my feelings and the interpretive information they provide, and then I let them go. If I hang on to them, then I am no longer examining current reality with a sense of current awareness. The situation may be similar to, but not the same as, the past that created the feelings.

In contrast, someone who is reactive, or reactionary, is driven by feelings, by circumstances, by conditions and by their environment. The way they think, feel and behave is dependent upon the behavior of others. They are, in other words, irresponsible for themselves.

You have seen it several times before in this book, but here it comes again:

There is always a choice.

You can choose to be proactive, living by the Responsibility Principle and the Commitment Principle, applying Formula A and the Full Spectrum Responsibility Model, practicing forgiveness, being centered, discovering and uncovering more of the I AM at your core, being Natural, love-based, courageous, countermanding fear-based responses and looking for win-win solutions. In short you can choose to be a proactive visionary.

Or you can choose to be reactive, living in fear, reacting from fear, being irresponsible for yourself and to others, holding on to resentments, living by your programmes that no longer serve, being uncentered, ignoring the I AM at your core and the power that you have in your inner mind if you would only tap into it, defining yourself by your issues and feelings. In short you can choose to be a fear based, issues driven reactionary.

These choices are not one off decisions, although at some point you will need to make a clear and conscious decision to become a proactive visionary leader in your life, if that is the way you want to live. After that, you will be faced by a myriad of choice points moment by moment, hour by hour, day by day.

Nor does the decision to live as a proactive visionary suddenly turn a switch in you to "on" so that you somehow immediately and miraculously become a proactive visionary. Instead, the decision is a commitment to strive, step by step to the best of your abilities at each moment in time, to move towards love and away from fear.

Each time you have a choice or a decision to make, and that is every moment of every day, you have the opportunity to make a conscious choice to move towards your I AM or away from your I AM, towards love or towards fear, towards proactivity or towards reactionism.

Many people live their lives oblivious to the fact that they are in fact making choices all the time. They go through life unaware and unconscious, reacting through their programmes and auto pilot. Perhaps they might make the same decisions even if they thought about it, but at least then it would be a conscious choice.

There is a simple little test to help you know when you are becoming more of a proactive visionary.

By choice, and in spite of the circumstances, and especially when the circumstances are difficult, you choose:

- Courtesy even if you are angry;
- Integrity, even if you are upset;
- Openness, even if you are afraid;
- Ethics, even when you are worried.

Life is short. For some, much shorter than they expect. Make each day count. Make your choices consciously. What do you want to have on your mind just before you die? Do you want to be full of regret for the unfulfilled potential of your life, for the resentments and the way you treated yourself and others? Do you want to feel joyful and satisfied that each day in every way you got better and better and better. That moment by moment, person by person, you made the world a better place.

So what do you want? How do you want to live? What do you want to be – a proactive visionary or a fear-based reactionary? If you haven't made that choice yet, now is the time. Do you want to be defined by your desires and vision of what you want or by your fear of what you don't want?

If you find yourself often being against things, for example, against poverty, against cruelty, against war, against discrimination, this is a sign that you are operating from a fear-based reaction stand point. A proactive visionary is for things… for a reduction in the discrepancy between the haves and have not's, for caring for the vulnerable whether they be people or animals, for peace, for equality. I challenge you to test this by looking at your social media. How do the "against" entries feel when you read them… the videos of cruelty or bad behaviour, the rants against this or that? Compare that with the "for" entries... the videos of rescued lab animals, the calls for positive action. I know what I skim over and what I take notice of!

How big an impact do you want to have with your life? How big an impact is possible with your life? Is it time that you started to think big, dream big and create an audacious vision for your life? It might be about your relationships, your family. Or about your career. Or is it about a philanthropic venture or adventure? What have you longed for? What has fear held you back from? The tools in this book give you what you need to create that vision and bring it to fruition.

A word of caution though, just because you have engaged in personal development by reading this book and implementing the tools, techniques and strategies, reading other books, going to seminars and workshops, doesn't mean to say that life won't continue to throw curve balls at you. What it does mean is that you will be so much better equipped to deal with whatever life circumstances come your way.

Living life at a higher level is about uncovering our own unique gifts and sharing them with the world. As we discover our gifts, we get a sense of our self-worth, the value we can bring to the world, whether that is on a global scale or in the context of our closest circle. Further, as we recognize our own unique value then we necessarily begin to recognize the unique value of everyone around us. We start to honour and value ourselves and in doing so we honour everyone else. And that honouring of others feeds back so that I honour myself more. And so it goes.

The gifts, that were evident as a child and young person, that you learned to contain or withhold to protect yourself, no longer need protecting. These are the gifts that will enable you to have your impact on the world and fulfill your purpose and potential. These gifts are not something that you have, they are who you really are, the true essence of you. And as you live life at a higher level, you manifest in the outside world more and more of who you truly are.

Can you bring to mind people who have inspired you over the years? Perhaps a parent or other family member, a teacher, someone from history or a well-known personality today. What did you learn from them? They may not even know that they taught you something or touched you in some way. I wonder how many people there are out there for whom you have done the same. And how many more you will touch as the ripple effect of you living life at a higher level moves out through the world.

One thing is for sure, we are not getting out of this lifetime alive. Time is passing. Second by second, minute by minute. And, whether you choose to be a proactive visionary or a fear based reactionary, time will continue to tick away. Is it time that you started to live with more of a sense of urgency, with more commitment to who you really are and what that means to your world?

As we choose proactive vision as our modus operandi, we honour ourselves and others and our consciousness rises. The definition of "others" expands from other people around us, to all people, to sentient beings, to the planet and ultimately to the universe. We start to recognize that every seemingly small decision we make has an impact. What we eat, what we drive, where we shop, what we wear, whether we smile and wave at our neighbour in the morning, how we speak to our children, our coworkers, or the person behind the cash register. Every choice we make has consequences.

As I bring this book to a close, I hope that you will choose to take on board the principles, tools and techniques set out here. I hope that you will make the decision to live your life as a proactive visionary moving step by step towards love and away from fear. The world certainly needs more proactivity and less fear-based living. Everything in this book has become part of who I am. It has changed my life for the better in so many ways, and it can do the same for you.

This is what I stand for:

There is always a choice.

Every choice has its consequences: consider them.

Each day in every way I am getting better and better and better.

I have already quoted a line from John Denver's song It's About Time. To close this chapter I would like to share all the words of that inspirational song.

It's About Time
There's a full moon over India and Gandhi lives again.
Who's to say you have to lose for someone else to win?
In the eyes of all the people, the look is much the same.
For the first is just the last one when you play a deadly game.

It's about time we realize it, we're all in this together.
It's about time we find out, it's all of us or none.
It's about time we recognize it, these changes in the weather.
It's about time, it's about changes, and it's about time.

There's a light in the Vatican window for all the world to see.
And a voice cries in the wilderness. Sometimes he speaks for me.
I suppose I love him most of all when he kneels to kiss the land.
With his lips upon our mother's breast, he makes his strongest
stand.
It's about time we start to see it, the earth is our only home.
It's about time we start to face it, we can't make it here all alone.
It's about time we start to listen to the voices in the wind.
It's about time, it's about changes and it's about time.

There's a man who is my brother, I just don't know his name.
But I know his home and family because I know we feel the
same.
And it hurts me when he's hungry and when his children cry.
I too am a father, that little one is mine.
It's about time we begin it, to turn the world around.
It's about time we start to make it, the dream we've always
known.
It's about time we start to live it, the family of man.
It's about time, it's about changes and it's about time.
It's about peace and it's about plenty and it's about time.
It's about you and me together, and it's about time.

John Denver 1943 - 1997

Epilogue: Where Are Claire & Doug Today?

As I write this, it is now three years and three weeks since Doug died. In some ways it seems like just a few weeks ago and in others it seems like lifetimes ago. I have made some big changes since he passed away.

Three weeks after he died I came to England to be with my family for a month. I had taken care of the immediate paperwork and other necessary items and decided I should go away for a while to get grounded with my family and recuperate a bit.

When I returned to Canada, I started to centre on what was next for me. One thing was clear; I needed to continue to earn a living. However, I could do that from almost anywhere. Did I want to stay in Kelowna? Perhaps return to Toronto where I have good friends and many acquaintances. Or was it time to return to the UK?

I walked the dog three times a day out in the fields and woods in the hills around my home. Being in nature was centering in itself. As I walked I would ask the Universe "What should I do now?" Admittedly, it was very early days after a bereavement to be looking at making life decisions, but I wanted, and needed, to start to at least consider my options.

As I walked through that beautiful countryside asking the Universe for direction and not getting an answer, I realised that the question I was asking was not the right question to get a helpful answer. I firmly believe that the quality of the answers we get depends crucially on the quality of the questions we ask.

So I started walking and asking "What question do I need to ask?"

It was only five months after Doug died that my father was diagnosed with cancer of the oesophagus. He was 84 and, thankfully, had been fit, well and active to that point. I travelled to the UK to spend some time with him when he was diagnosed. As I sat on the tarmac at Kelowna airport in a little Dash 8 aircraft waiting to take off to get my connection to fly Transatlantic, all of a sudden, from nowhere a question popped into my head. No, not **a** question, **the** question: "If I never saw the people in Canada again how much would it matter? If I never saw the people in the UK again how much would it matter?" Finally, the right question and, in that instant, with absolute clarity, I knew that I needed to move back to the UK. I also knew, not in my head, but in my inner mind, that my father was going to die in a short time. I decided to tell him and the rest of my family that I was planning to move back to the UK, but not to act upon it until he had passed. I didn't want selling a property and getting ready for an international move to get in the way of spending time supporting my father and step mother through the next few months.

My father passed away at the end of January 2012. When I returned to Canada after his funeral I began to put things in motion for my move. At the end of June 2012 I landed back in the UK.

So where am I now? I am living in a small rural community in North Lincolnshire within an easy drive of family and old friends. My dog, who accompanied me on those questioning walks in Kelowna, continues to be my faithful companion having made the Transatlantic journey herself at the age of 12!

I continue to enjoy lots of variety in my work and life. I have my analytical consulting projects as well as the Full Spectrum Life work. I have been welcomed into the community and made some good connections here.

Doug and I used to ballroom dance together. I loved it and was determined not to lose that part of my life because I had lost my partner. So I continue to ballroom dance and continue to love it. I may even get to dance at the Winter Gardens in Blackpool this October. Now if I can do that, you can do anything you want to do!

Bottom line is, although I wish the circumstances were different and that Doug was still here, I accept that he isn't, I rejoice in his presence in my life in all the ways he makes himself known to me, I choose to be engaged with the world and I choose to be happy.

Doug, of course, is not here in the physical sense. But he lives on in his continuing influence on my life and work, through his son and through the lives of all the people he touched throughout his life.

At the same time as he wrote the piece about his early life presented in Chapter 1, Doug also wrote a poem about his life.

Whilst he had not shared the prose part of his writing with me, he did show me this poem when he wrote it. I believe that he also intended this to be part of his book, and so here it is:

The Sandbox

My sandbox is a tear-filled puddle,
Don't know what caused all the trouble,
Wading through the issues with my life,
Leaving them here, all toil and strife.

My sandbox is a tear filled puddle,
Mindful awareness, wandering muddle,
Observer watches "who am I",
Peeking through to sun-filled sky.

My sandbox is a tear filled puddle,
Draining dry, grit and stubble,
Slaying demons, new found might,
Feeling, sensing, finding right.

My sandbox was a tear-filled puddle,
Playing softly, personal huddle,
Tentative, open, feeling light,
Stretching, reaching far to higher heights.

Doug Cameron 1954-2011

A Final Word From Doug

Doug spent his last six weeks in Kelowna Hospice House. A truly remarkable place. I will be eternally grateful to the staff and volunteers. There are many special times that I remember from those six weeks. One in particular stands out. He hadn't spoken a full sentence for about four weeks. Just "yes" and "no". Because of where the tumour was in his brain, his cognitive abilities were impacted. At this point I didn't even know whether he comprehended that he was going to die very soon.

He and I were sitting out in the garden enjoying the early spring sunshine and the peace and quiet of the hospice garden. We could see the mountains in the distance still capped in snow. As we sat quietly together, I commented on how beautiful it was there, not expecting any more than maybe getting a "yes" from him. Instead, this is what he said:

*"It's the end of the world. Good place to spend
the last days."*

It was another three weeks before he died, but this was the last sentence he said, the last thought he expressed verbally.

May you find that kind of peace and acceptance in your everyday life.

Acknowledgements

There are so many people to acknowledge in terms of their influence on me and the fact that this book has been written. I believe that everything in life is a preparation for something coming in the future. In that context, everyone who has ever been a part of my life, whether I felt positive or negative about it at the time, should be acknowledged and thanked for helping to bring me to the point of completing this book. So to all of you... thank you!

I am going to highlight some of the people most closely connected with me, the book and the events it portrays.

My family and step family have always been a great source of comfort and encouragement. Most especially, my mother, **Barbara Safford**, my late father, **John Safford**, my step mother, **Dorothy Safford**, my sister, **Stephanie Wall** and my brother, **Robert Safford**. Then there are my brother-in-law, **David Wall**, my sister-in-law, **Karen Safford**, and my niece and nephew, **Lucy and James Safford**. We don't necessarily live in close proximity or have day in and day out involvement in each other's lives, but we do know that we can always count on each other if the need arises. In recent years, I have also had the chance to get to know, and thoroughly enjoy the company of, my cousin **Michael Grant**. My step sisters, **Jane Perry** and **Diane Garner**, and my step brother, **Tim Goodlad**, and their families have shown me what a big family is all about, always welcoming me to be part of their extended network of cousins, nieces and nephews.

Acknowledgments of family members would not be complete without mentioning a number of family friends going way back to childhood days. They became the extended family that we didn't have: "aunts", "uncles" and "cousins"... **Mary Hanson**, the late **Bob Hanson** and their daughters **Julie and Linda**. **Pauline Houghton**, the late **Jim Houghton** and their daughters **Jane and Julie**. **Denis and Irene Goodchild** and their son **Stephen**, sadly all gone now.

I am blessed to have my own step son, **Christopher Cameron**. He and I got on happily together from the first time we met when he was 12. He is an intelligent, kind and loyal man and such a clear reminder to me of his father. He embodies Doug's legacy in such an honourable way.

I am so grateful that Christopher's mother, **Karin Nitsche**, and I have become friends. Karin is a gentle soul who has experienced great suffering and yet manages to keep sharing her inherent joyfulness with the world. The environment she created for Christopher as he grew up is a major factor in who he is today.

There are three special friends who have seen me through some of the best and worst times of my life. **Alan Hedges**, **Antoniette Berenguer** and **Caroline Schweppe**.

I met Alan in university when I was 19. We have had some laughs! Miraculously, Alan and his wife moved to Detroit just three weeks after I moved to Toronto. I am honoured to be god-mother to all three of Alan's children: **Christina, Robert and Amanda**. We have had some great fun together and he has supported me through tough times too. He has always been a steadfast friend, but took that to a whole new level during

Doug's illness and the weeks after his death. In a life already so full, he managed to make time to call me every single day. He made the trip from Pittsburgh to Kelowna to see us when Doug was diagnosed with the brain tumour. He came again for the weekend of my first birthday without Doug. My thanks go not just to Alan, but also to his wife, **Dids**, for having the grace to let him be such an important support to me.

Antoniette and I met at a Lifestream seminar in 1995. She was a volunteer team leader and I was fortunate to be in her team. Our friendship grew from that experience together. We have also shared some of the best and worst of times. She is such a positive person, always thinking of others, finding ways to encourage and uplift, setting such a marvelous example for her family and those lucky enough to be in her life. I have such fond memories of Doug and I being welcomed into the Berenguer home as part of the wedding celebrations for both of her sons. Right now she is showing great courage and positivity as she goes through cancer treatment.

Caroline Schweppe was one of the first people I met when I moved to Canada in 1990. She worked for the same company as I did in a different department. Caroline is from Dublin originally and we hit it off right away. Who wouldn't with such a fun-loving, out-going, intelligent woman? As we matured and went through the ups and downs of life, Caroline and I became great support for each other. I value Caroline's insight into people so highly. She is a natural leader and a communicator extraordinaire.

The late **Jim Quinn** gave so much to Doug... the first glimmer of hope that life could be better, the example of a gentle, loving and firm father figure, the opportunity to "apprentice" to him as a facilitator, and his blessing to take flight as a solo facilitator of personal development. Also, I want to acknowledge Jim for the time and wisdom he shared with me during Doug's "apprenticeship" as well as my own life changing experiences in his Lifestream workshops.

My colleague and friend, the late **Dennis Nicolls**, took me on as his "project" and got me to my first Lifestream workshop.

Our (now my) business partners, **Peter Comrie** and **Joyce Evans** without whom I don't believe Doug would have had the chance to fulfill his dream of facilitating the Full Spectrum Leadership Intensive. He achieved this dream just ten weeks before he died. Joyce's calm and centered energy is infectious. Peter is a powerhouse of ideas and enthusiasm. His friendship was highly valued by Doug, and I will never forget the constant help, support and just being there Peter provided during the last weeks of Doug's life.

Four people selflessly gave up a week of their time and a huge amount of their energy, skills and commitment, to travel from the four corners of North America to volunteer as team leaders at the Full Spectrum Leadership Intensive in March 2011. Lives were changed that week. It turned out to be Doug's swan song. It was a dream fulfilled for him and it would not have been possible without **Antoniette and John Berenguer, Dalyce Comm** and **Michael Giddings**.

Thank you to **all the grads of Full Spectrum Leadership workshops, as well as the New Leaf and Eppica programmes** before them, for placing their trust in us to guide them through the unique experience that is breakthrough experiential personal development training. Many have inspired me. Many have gone on to inspire others, making a difference in their lives by living the Full Spectrum principles.

My move to Canada and all the adventures, twists and turns that lead to, including this book, would not have happened if it hadn't been for my partner at the time, **Mike Lynch**. I don't think I would have had the courage to make a move like that alone. With Mike at my side, and equally excited about making a life there, it was easy. Ultimately, we went our separate ways and continued our own Canadian odysseys.

Another source of learning, support and friendship for me since 2004 is the ordained and lay Sangha of the New Kadampa Tradition. There are three people from that group who stand out for special acknowledgement. **Gen Kelsang Sanden, Gen Kelsang Delek and Kelsang Chenma**. The three of them played pivotal roles in our lives in BC and in Doug's illness and passing. Being a recipient of their friendship, joyfulness, wisdom, compassion and clarity of mind is a great honour and blessing to me. Gen Kelsang Sanden and Doug were like the best kind of brothers you could imagine. They loved each other dearly.

I can't say enough about the **Kelowna Hospice House** and the difference it made to Doug's last six weeks of life. The building itself is inspiring. The people who work and volunteer there are remarkable. Those six weeks were perhaps the most profound experience of my life so far. An experience made possible by the vision and determination of the people who drove the campaign to build the hospice in the first place, all the fundraisers and donors, large and small, who make sure that the hospice is able to continue is vital work, all the staff and

171

volunteers past and present. The staff cheerfully welcomed the great variety of visitors Doug and I had at the hospice. I would like to acknowledge two of the nurses in particular, **Bo** and **Bern**, and one of the volunteers, who is also a friend, **Wendy Gillett**.

There were several other people who played their part in making my life in those six weeks as hassle free and supported as possible:

Paul, Lexie and the staff at A1 Boarding Kennels loved and looked after our dog, Cassie, for the last three weeks when I needed to be at the hospice more and more and for a month when I came to the UK to recuperate after Doug's death. She had spent many happy holidays with them before those difficult times and the parting when we moved to the UK was emotional.

My neighbours, **Tony and Winnie Sousa**, also took care of Cassie. Winnie walked her every morning until she had to go to Paul and Lexie. Another neighbour, **Donna McEvoy**, was such a kind presence. She had worked as a nurse in palliative care for many years and gave me helpful and informed advice and knowledge. My other neighbour, **Bonnie Pisio**, was also a great friend and support through that time, including being part of the garden crew.

Two very special ladies from the Full Spectrum Leadership grads, **Arden Rutherford** and **Elena Tsykova**, brought beautiful organic, raw food to the hospice every day to supplement Doug's hospice food diet and make sure I was getting good nutrition too. The staff would come by his room after Arden or Elena had been, to see what goodies we had that day. I think Doug's two favourites were Arden's raw chocolate pudding and Elena's Russian eggs.

A big group of **Kelowna Full Spectrum Leadership grads** spent an afternoon, in awful weather, doing the spring clean-up of our garden. Despite the rain, they were happy, cheerful, singing and did a marvelous job that was just too much for me to deal with at that time. My garden is my haven and it upsets me when it is not looked after, so that afternoon of work they all did was much more than just a physical tidy up, it gave me peace and contentment. A special thanks to **Riel Marquardt** who made a very moving video of interviews with people as they went about their work that afternoon. You can see the video at http://www.fullspectrumleadership.ca/leadership-team/claire-cameron/doug-cameron/. Riel also spent time with Doug at the hospice. He brought his calm, peaceful, centered energy to Doug's room and sat quietly with him. Words were not necessary between them.

Thank you to the people who helped to bring this book to fruition by reviewing and commenting on drafts: my dear friend, gifted healer and businesswoman, **Anne Reid**, my sister (need I say more), **Stephanie Wall**, my business partner and huge supporter during Doug's illness, **Peter Comrie**, and Doug's long-time friend and best man at our wedding, **Keith Tarswell**.

Thanks also to my friend **Daisa Morgan**. Daisa's friendship and wisdom were instrumental in my recuperation after Doug and my father's deaths, and my move to the UK.

My friend, **Eleana Pinglo**, has also made my transition to living back in the UK that much easier. Her constant optimism is an inspiration to me.

Finally, I would like to acknowledge the role that three ballroom dance teachers in particular have played. Doug and I started ballroom dancing at the Oakville Fred Astaire studio. We had some great teachers there and enjoyed ourselves so much. We laughed and laughed during those lessons. When we got to Kelowna it took us five years to find a teacher that we connected with. We were so blessed to eventually find **Chris Thorburn** of Kelowna Ballroom. Chris is such an experienced dancer and an exceptional teacher. The group we danced with was so supportive during Doug's illness. Chris became a friend and I remember the days he used to come to the hospice at lunchtime to visit with us. The hardest thing about leaving Kelowna was leaving Chris and the group of dancers he taught. After Doug died, I had the courage to go back to dance classes alone, without a partner, because I knew that Chris and the class would welcome me there and support me in my wish to continue dancing.

That gave me the courage to start going to classes here in the UK by myself, without a partner. **Sophie Brooke** was the first teacher I went to. She has welcomed me into her classes despite being partnerless! Sophie is a lovely young woman, a talented dancer and another exceptional teacher.

I was then introduced to another teacher and group of dancers where, lo and behold, a gentleman was looking for a dance partner! Now, I have a lot of catching up to do to dance at his level, but I am loving the process of doing that with our teacher **Nigel Scott**.

I suspect that these three teachers don't really understand the depth of the impact they have had on the rebuilding of my life after Doug's death. Two of them never even knew him. But I am convinced that they are integral to my mental and emotional health as I build a new life, making new connections and redefining myself.

Doug has been with me as I have written this book. As I typed I could often hear him speaking the words. I hope I have done justice to what he wanted to create but ran out of time to do.

References, Resources and Influences

All the books referenced in the text are listed here along with other books and seminars that have provided me with resources and influenced my thinking and approach to personal development. The list is by no means exhaustive. I would be here for a very long time if I managed to capture all the books that have impacted me.

The Arbinger Institute: Leadership and Self Deception, 2010, Berrett-Koehler Publishers, ISBN 978-1-57675-977-6

Bly, Robert: Iron John, 1990, Addison-Wesley Publishing Company, ISBN 0-201-51720-5

Cameron, Doug: EPPICA Journey workshop

Cameron, Doug: Full Spectrum Leadership Basic workshop

Cameron, Doug: Full Spectrum Leadership Intensive workshop

Clemmer, Jim: Growing the Distance - Timeless Principles for Personal, Career and Family Success, TCG Press, 1999, ISBN 0-9684675-0-4,

Covey, Stephen R: Principle-Centered Leadership, Simon & Schuster, 1990, ISBN 0-671-79280-6

Covey, Stephen R: The 7 Habits of Highly Successful People, Simon & Schuster, 1989, ISBN 0-671-70863-5

Einstein, Albert: Fear and Longing, New York Times, 1930

Enright, Robert D and Fitzgibbons, Richard P: Helping Clients Forgive - An Empirical Guide for Resolving Anger and

Restoring Hope, American Psychological Association, 2000, ISBN-10 1-557-98689-4

Everett, Alexander: Inward Bound – Living Life From the Inside Out, Bookpartners, 1998, ISBN-10 1-8852-2176-2

Geshe Kelsang Gyatso: Writings and teachings. Published by Tharpa

Frankl, Victor: Man's Search for Meaning, Simon & Schuster, 1959, ISBN 0-671-24422-1

Frankl, Victor: Man's Search for Ultimate Meaning, Perseus Publishing, 2000, ISBN 0-7382-0354-8

Hicks, Esther and Jerry (The Teachings of Abraham): Ask and It Is Given, Hay House, 2010, ISBN-10 1-4019-0459-9

Hicks, Esther and Jerry (The Teachings of Abraham): The Amazing Power of Deliberate Intent, Hay House, 2006, ISBN-10 1-4019-0696-6

Hicks, Esther and Jerry (The Teachings of Abraham): The Astonishing Power of Emotions, Hay House, 2007, ISBN 978-1-4019-1246-8

Hill, Napoleon: Think and Grow Rich, Palmera Publishing, 1937, ISBN-10 1-456-31695-8

Jeffers, Susan: Feel the Fear and do it Anyway: How to Turn Your Fear and Indecision into Confidence and Action, Arrow, 1993, ISBN-10 0-099-74100-8

Mandino, Og: The Choice, Bantam, 1920, ISBN-10 0-553-24576-7

Millman, Dan: The Life You Were Born to Live, H J Kramer, 1993, ISBN-10 0-915-81160-X

Pausch, Randy: The Last Lecture, Hyperion, 2008, ISBN 978-1-4013-2325-7

Quinn, James Rosswell (Ross): The Love Based Leader - Creating Success by Overcoming Fear-based Living, Quinn Incorporated, 2011, ISBN-10 1-451-55644-6,

Quinn, Jim: Lifestream Basic Seminar

Quinn, Ross: Leadershape Seminar

Quinn, Ross: Lifestream IPI Seminar

Quinn, Ross: The People Wheel Audio Programme

Robbins, Anthony: Unleash the Power Within Seminar

Robbins, Anthony: Get the Edge Audio Programme

Stearn, Jess: The Power of Alpha Thinking, William Morrow and Company, 1976

Thich Nhat Hanh: Peace Is Every Step, Bantam, 1991, ISBN 0-553-35139-7

Tolle, Eckhart: A New Earth – Awakening to Your Life's Purpose, Penguin, 2005, ISBN 978-0-452-28996-3

Waitley, Denis: The Psychology of Winning, Warner Books, 1992

Wattles, Wallace D: The Science of Being Great, first published by Elizabeth Towne Company, 1910

Wattles, Wallace D: The Science of Being Well, first published by Elizabeth Towne Company, 1910

Wattles, Wallace D: The Science of Getting Rich, first published by Elizabeth Towne Company, 1910

Williamson, Marianne: A Return to Love - Reflections on the Principles of A Course in Miracles, Thorsons, 1996,

ISBN-10 0-722-53299-7

FOUR
PILLARS

HEALTH, WEALTH, RELATIONSHIPS
AND CONTRIBUTION

www.FullSpectrumLife.org